THE EVERYTHING KIDS' SOCCER BOOK

2ND EDITION

Rules, techniques, and more about your favorite sport!

Deborah W. Crisfield

Aadamsmedia

avon, massachusetts

PUBLISHER Karen Cooper

DIRECTOR OF ACQUISITIONS AND INNOVATION Paula Munier

MANAGING EDITOR, EVERYTHING SERIES Lisa Laing

COPY CHIEF Casey Ebert

ACQUISITIONS EDITOR Katrina Schroeder

SENIOR DEVELOPMENT EDITOR Brett Palana-Shanahan

EDITORIAL ASSISTANT Hillary Thompson

An Everything® Series Book.
Everything® and everything.com® are registered trademarks of F+W Media, Inc.

Published by Adams Media, a division of F+W Media, Inc.
57 Littlefield Street, Avon, MA 02322. U.S.A.
www.adamsmedia.com

ISBN 10: 1-60550-162-X
ISBN 13: 978-1-60550-162-8

Printed by RR Donnelley, Harrisonburg, VA, USA.
December 2013

10   9   8   7   6   5

This publication is designed to provide accurate and authoritative information with regard to the subject matter covered. It is sold with the understanding that the publisher is not engaged in rendering legal, accounting, or other professional advice. If legal advice or other expert assistance is required, the services of a competent professional person should be sought.
—From a *Declaration of Principles* jointly adopted by a Committee of the American Bar Association and a Committee of Publishers and Associations

Many of the designations used by manufacturers and sellers to distinguish their products are claimed as trademarks. When those designations appear in this book and Adams Media was aware of a trademark claim, the designations have been printed with initial capital letters.

Interior illustrations by Kurt Dolber.
Puzzles by Beth L. Blair

This book is available at quantity discounts for bulk purchases.
For information, please call 1-800-289-0963.

Visit the entire Everything® series at *www.everything.com*

Dedication

This book is dedicated to the Summit Charge

Acknowledgments

I'd like to thank Laura Madden for her coaching skills, Rob Stone for his knowledge, Carrie Finizio for her connections, the Summit Charge for their inspiring play, and JAC, JDC, and CBC for keeping it fun, as always.

Contents

Introduction

Soccer can be found in more countries than any other sport in the world, and no other game is played by more people. It's the fastest growing sport in the United States, and it's the second most popular game for kids in this country (behind basketball). Yes, soccer is on top of the world, and you are on top of this exciting trend.

This book will help you become a super soccer player. If you've never played before, you'll get step-by-step instructions on every skill. And if you've already spent some time on the ball, the games and drills will help you improve your skills.

The first chapter covers some of the history of soccer and all of the rules, field markings, and equipment. If you're a little confused about the offside rule, look in Chapter 1.

The skills begin in Chapter 2. This is where you'll learn how to control the ball, the first step for any soccer player. Passing skills and strategy are discussed in Chapter 3, and dribbling is in Chapter 4. By the time you've read this far, you should be able to move the ball down the field like a pro.

There are a few among you who are daredevils, I'm sure. You folks don't mind being the center of attention, diving on the ground, and jumping hard into a group of attackers. You are goalkeepers. From cutting the angle to stopping the toughest of shots—all of the essential goal-tending info is in Chapter 5.

Once you've learned to move the ball, it's time to develop your soccer brain. You need to know how to think like a soccer player. Chapters 6 and 7 help you understand field positions and strategies, from attack through the midfield and on to defense.

Of course, playing soccer is all about having fun, being healthy, and enjoying yourself. Chapter 8 will help you stay fit and avoid injuries, and Chapter 9 covers all levels of soccer, from pick-up games to the World Cup.

And, of course, every chapter is filled with puzzles, jokes, games, and other fun things for you to do while you learn about the world's favorite sport. Kick back and enjoy!

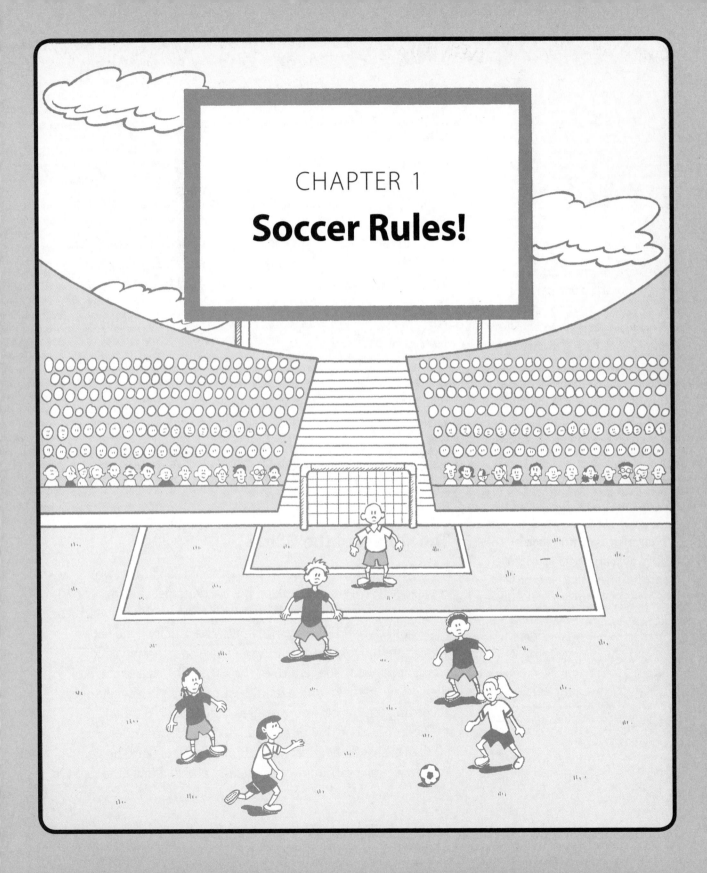

kay, so you know that soccer rules, but what are the soccer rules?

Soccer is about as simple as it gets. To play, you need a field, two goals, and a ball. That's it. The goals don't even have to be official goals. Cones, T-shirts, even a couple of trees will do the trick.

And talk about easy! Basically, it's no hands allowed, and kick the ball into the opponent's goal. Pretty simple, huh? Think about the rules for soccer compared to the rules for baseball or football. Even three-year-olds can learn the basic rules of soccer, but there are many grownups who still can't figure out baseball.

But if you've caught the soccer bug, you'll probably want to know a few more rules than the average three-year-old. Like, what's the deal with the offside rule? And how do you do a kickoff? And what are those yellow and red cards I keep hearing about?

Read on for the answers, but don't worry. Soccer really is still as simple as you thought it was.

The Object of the Game

Go for the goal! That's the whole point of the game. Two teams, each with a goal to defend, battle to get the soccer ball into the opponent's goal. The winning team is the one with the most goals when the time runs out. The official time is two 45-minute halves, but most leagues use shorter halves for younger players. The length of the game, the size of the ball, the size of the field, and even the number of players changes according to how old you are. (See the table on page 4.)

Soccer is played with one ball and two teams of eleven players each: ten field players and one goalkeeper. The goalkeeper wears a different colored shirt and is allowed to use his

FUN FACT

Ancient History

Soccer is one of the oldest sports in the world. No one is quite sure when or where it started. China was the first country to actually write about a game that involved kicking a round object into a goal, and that game was played more than 4,000 years ago! The game was called *tsu chu,* and it was played for the emperor's birthday.

More Ancient History

In England during the time of knights and castles, whole towns would play a game like soccer. The ball would be anything that rolled and the goals could be close (if only a few people were playing) or as much as ten miles apart if hundreds of people played.

or her hands to touch the ball. The ten field players generally fall into one of three categories:

- **Defenders**—Keep the ball from getting into the goal
- **Midfielders**—Provide a link between defenders and forwards
- **Attackers**—Shoot the ball into the opponent's goal

As you can see, each position has a job to do. You'll find more detailed descriptions in Chapters 6 and 7.

Having a Ball

Thousands of years ago, a soccer ball could be anything, as long as it was round and it rolled. Here are some things that people used for soccer balls:

- Animal skins filled with grass
- Coconuts
- Human skulls
- Pigs' bladders

Today, in many poorer countries, soccer players still have to make their own soccer balls. What would you use if you didn't have a soccer ball? List three things around your house that might make a good soccer ball.

_____

_____

_____

Soccer balls come in many sizes and in several different designs. The traditional ball is called a Size 5 ball and consists

FUN FACT

Slight Change in Plans

Many younger teams play with seven, eight, or nine on a side. Because younger players haven't learned to spread out, this makes the field less crowded. It also gives each player more opportunities to touch the ball.

of thirty-two leather panels: twelve are pentagonal (five-sided) and twenty are hexagonal (six-sided). It's about 27 inches in diameter and weighs about 15 ounces.

You'll use a Size 4 ball, a Size 5 ball, and maybe a Size 3 ball in your soccer-playing career. The following table shows how ball size, field size, goal size, and length of the game change according to how old you are. Every league has its own guidelines, but most of them will be close to these numbers.

AGE	BALL SIZE	FIELD SIZE	GOAL SIZE	LENGTH OF GAME
Under 6	3	20 x 30 yds.	4 x 6 ft.	20-minute halves
Under 8	3	30 x 50 yds.	6 x 12 ft.	20-minute halves
Under 10	4	50 x 70 yds.	6 x 18 to 7 x 21 ft.	25-minute halves
Under 11–Under 17	5	100 x 50 to 120 x 80 yds.	8 yds. x 8 ft.	30-45 minute halves
High school, college, pro	5	same	same	45-minute halves

If you're interested in soccer, you'll definitely want to get your own ball. Nothing will help your soccer playing more than getting used to how the ball bounces around your foot.

The Field of Play

The size of a soccer field is flexible. Remember, back in the Middle Ages, the goals could be as far as 10 miles apart. The rules are a little more rigid now, but fields can still be different sizes.

Officially, the field should be between 100 and 130 yards long, and between 50 and 100 yards wide. But you could never have a square field; that is, 100 by 100. The length always has to be longer than the width. The goal is 8 yards wide and 8 feet high. Take a look at the following picture to see all the measurements.

Even though these are the official measurements, you might be playing on a much smaller field. If you're playing on a team that has fewer than eleven on a side, then you *definitely* will be.

Like in the Good Old Days

For a fun variation on soccer, try to play the way they did in olden times. Go to a park near your house and set up two goals, one on each side of the park. Try to get as many people involved as you can and see what fun it is to have to dribble and pass around trees, playground equipment, and backstops.

4

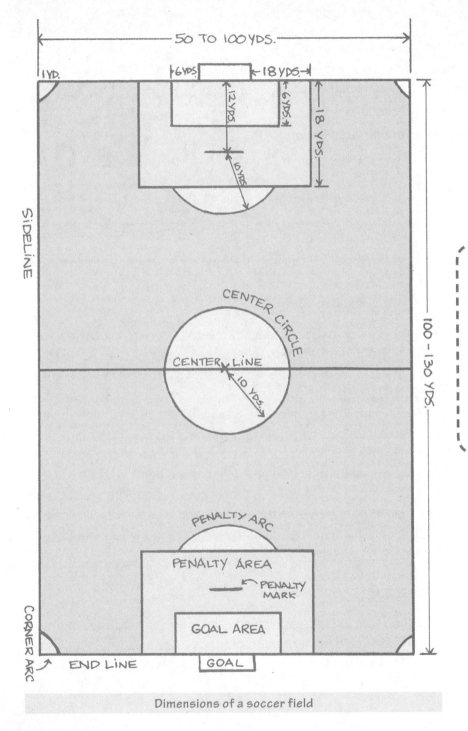

50 TO 100 YDS.

1 YD.

6 YDS.

18 YDS.

12 YDS.

6 YDS.

18 YDS.

10 YDS.

100 – 130 YDS.

SIDELINE

CENTER CIRCLE

CENTER LINE

10 YDS.

PENALTY ARC

PENALTY AREA

PENALTY MARK

GOAL AREA

CORNER ARC

END LINE

GOAL

Dimensions of a soccer field

FUN FACT

The Big Field

The official size for an international match is a field that is 100 to 110 meters long (which is 110 to 120 yards) and 64 to 75 meters wide (which is 70 to 80 yards).

Spelling Ball

How many words can you find in this soccer ball grid? You may start at any letter, then move from space to the next touching space in any direction, spelling out a word as you go. You may double back and use a letter more than once in a word (you can spell "eve"), but you may not use the same letter twice in a row (you can't spell "sleep").

The 10-letter BONUS word completes this phrase: Playing soccer is much more fun than watching _____!

SCORE:
10 words = Starter
20 words = Pro
30 words = World Cup

Dressing the Part

If you're on a team, you'll probably be given a uniform. Then it's your job to round out the whole outfit with cleats and shin guards. Cleats are leather shoes with small rubber knobs on the bottom that keep you from sliding on the grass. Shin guards are hard plastic shields that you strap onto the lower part of your leg to keep your shins from getting bruised or even broken.

Playing the Game

Once the ball is in play, the teams try to move the ball up the field toward the opponent's goal. A player may move the ball with any part of his body except for the parts between the shoulders and the fingertips. A player can keep the ball or pass it off to another player. The team without the ball does its best to steal the ball and stop the opponents from shooting.

Play is only stopped when the ball goes into the goal or rolls out-of-bounds (the entire ball must be beyond the outer edge of the line) or when a foul is committed. Play can also be stopped by the referee for any reason he or she determines. The clock is never stopped, unless there is a serious injury.

Restarts

Whenever the referee blows his whistle, play stops. It might be because the ball went out of bounds or because a player committed a foul. And of course, once play has stopped, it has to start again, and there are lots of different ways to do this—all depending on why play was stopped in the first place. These are called restarts or set plays.

The Kickoff

Kickoffs are used for three different events.

1. At the start of a game
2. At the start of the second half
3. After a goal has been scored

The ball is placed in the center of the center circle. Each team must start the game on their side of the field. The defending team must also stay out of the center circle. The other team has at least one and often two players up near the ball. At the referee's whistle, the game begins. The ball is moved and then it's up for grabs. The player who kicked the ball first may not touch it again until someone else has touched it.

Throw-Ins

When a player kicks the ball over a touchline (sideline), the other team gets to throw the ball back in. It's the one time you are allowed to touch the ball with your hands as a field player. But don't just wind up and give it a toss. There are a lot of rules you must follow.

1. Both feet must be on the ground when you let go of the ball.
2. You must throw the ball equally with both hands.
3. Both hands must start from behind your head and come all the way over.
4. Your body must face the way you're throwing.

The throw-in

Most new players have a hard time learning how to do the throw-in properly. You can read the rules and look at the following picture, but the best thing to do is to get outside with a friend and practice it. Make sure you have someone watch you, though, because you don't want to be practicing an incorrect throw!

Goal Kicks

When the attacking team kicks the ball over the goal line (the end line), the defending team gets a free kick. This is called a goal kick. Sometimes new players call this a "goalie" kick. That's not right. In fact, at the lower levels of soccer, the goalie (or keeper) is the last player who should be taking this kick! The kick might not go very far and you want the keeper in the goal protecting it from whatever is coming back at you.

For a goal kick, the ball should be placed anywhere within the six-yard box, but most players put it on the corner of the box. You'll want to do this, too, because that spot gets you closest to the sideline and the farthest away from your goal. You need every advantage you can get.

Touchline: Also known as the sideline. One of the two longer lines that are the boundaries of the field of play. The lines are included as part of the field of play.

Goal line: Also known as the endline. One of the two shorter lines that form the boundaries of the field of play. The lines are included as part of the field.

Tip

If you're defending the goal and can choose whether to kick the ball out over the touchline or the goal line, always choose the touchline. A corner kick is a much bigger advantage to the other team than a throw-in.

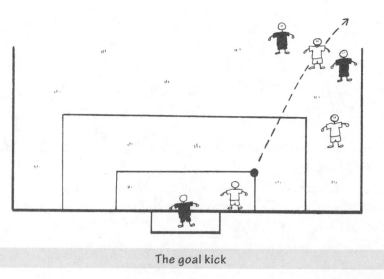

The goal kick

Corner Kicks

If the defenders kick the ball over their own goal line, something very different happens. It's called a corner kick. The attacking team places the ball in the corner of the field, where the touchline and the goal line meet.

The ball can go directly into the goal on a corner kick, though it takes a rather talented kicker to manage that.

Make sure you pay attention to the referee's whistle. You don't want to pick up a ball that you think is over the line when it's really not. Otherwise, the other team gets a free kick because of your "handball." And keep in mind, a ball is not out-of-bounds until it has rolled completely over the line. If it's still touching part of the line, then it's still in play.

The corner kick

Foul Play

While there are few rules to the game of soccer, there are guidelines to keep play safe and fair. When you play, you'll have one, two, or three referees. These refs will make the out-of-bounds calls and blow the whistle for fouls.

FUN FACT

It's the Ref's Call

There are times when a referee might not call an obvious foul. This usually happens when the team that is fouled has the advantage after the foul is committed. For instance, if they were about to score, it would be unfair to stop play and set up a free kick just because the other team fouled. In fact, it might encourage some players to behave badly and try to foul whenever the other team gets close to the goal.

There are a whole bunch of actions that will cause a referee to blow her whistle. See how many you can name. If you get one or two, you're a soccer starter; three or four, you're a soccer smarty; five or more, you're a soccer star. Don't peek at the list until you've tried it yourself.

◆ Charging
◆ Touching the ball with your hands
◆ Hitting
◆ Holding
◆ Kicking
◆ Pushing
◆ Tripping

◆ Dangerous play (like a high kick near someone's head)
◆ Goalkeeper offenses
◆ Interfering with the goalkeeper
◆ Obstruction
◆ Violating the offside rule
◆ Ungentlemanly conduct (bad behavior)

Those are the main ones. If a player commits one of these fouls, the other team gets a free kick. There are a few other minor fouls, but they probably won't be an issue for you unless you go pro.

Notice that the fouls are divided into two groups. For the first group of fouls, the team gets a direct kick. A direct kick means that the team can kick it right into the goal without anyone but the kicker touching the ball. If the player commits one of these fouls in the penalty box, look out! It's time for a penalty kick. Not only can the player kick it directly into the goal, but he gets to do it from a mere 12 yards away, and the other team is allowed no defense but the keeper.

The fouls in the second group are not quite as serious, so the team gets an indirect kick. That means that at least two players need to touch the ball before it goes into the goal.

WORDS to KNOW

Obstruction: This call means that you've placed your body between your opponent and the ball without going after the ball yourself. You might be trying to keep your opponent from saving the ball if it's going out-of-bounds or to give your keeper a chance to pick it up. Either way, it's not allowed. You *can* throw your body in front of another player, as long as you are actually going after the ball.

Pick a Card

If a player displays really bad behavior, is not playing fairly, or continues to commit the same foul again and again, the referee might pull out his cards. He has two cards: one yellow and one red. Think of them like a stoplight. The yellow one is a "slow down" or a warning that the red one isn't far behind. The referee makes a note of the player's number, and in many leagues, the coaches are required to put in a sub for that player. After a few minutes on the bench, the player can go back in.

Here are a few reasons you'll get a yellow card from a referee:

◆ Exceptionally rough fouls
◆ Holding an opponent
◆ Unsportsmanlike behavior
◆ Arguing with the referee
◆ Entering the field without the referee's permission
◆ Blocking the keeper
◆ Refusal to move the proper distance away from a free kick

If a player gets a second yellow card, then the red card comes out. Here are some other things that will get you an automatic red card:

◆ Violence
◆ Spitting
◆ Blocking a goal with your hands if you're not the keeper (which also gives the team an automatic goal)
◆ Bad language
◆ Receiving a second yellow card in the same game
◆ Denying an obvious goal-scoring chance by committing an intentional foul

FUN FACT

Red Cards Aplenty

In a match in Paraguay on June 1, 1993, a referee gave twenty players a red card and sent them off the field. They had to stop the game due to lack of players.

JOKIN' AROUND

An angry midfielder snarled at the referee. "What would happen if I called you a blind idiot who couldn't make the right call to save his life?"

"That would be a red card for you."

"And if I didn't say it but only thought it?"

"That's different. If you only thought it but didn't say anything, I couldn't do a thing."

"Well, we'll leave it like that, then, shall we?" smiled the player.

The red card means that the player is kicked off the field and he can't come back in. Not only that, but the team doesn't get to put in a sub either. In addition, the player may not be able to play in the next game as well, depending on the league rules.

What on Earth Is Offsides?

And now you've reached the point in the rules where you get to learn about the offsides rule. Offsides is a complicated rule but a good one. Without the offsides rule, teams would be able to have a player stand down near the other team's goal and just wait for the ball to come. Scoring a goal wouldn't be nearly as challenging.

Let's Play

In each of the soccer balls is the scrambled name of something you need to play soccer—minus one letter! Add the missing letter to complete the word. Then arrange the missing letters to spell one more important piece of soccer equipment.

1.
2.
3.
4.
5.
6.

1. O C K
2. E F D I
3. E E R Y R
4. L A B
5. M A
6. L W E I H T

1. _____
2. _____
3. _____
4. _____
5. _____
6. _____
BONUS: _____

So here's the nitty-gritty on the offsides rule. There are basically just two hard-and-fast rules to remember:

1. It can only happen on your opponent's half of the field. You can't be offsides if you're not over the middle line (in other words, closer to your goal than theirs).
2. Once you cross the midfield line, you must keep either the ball or two opponents (the keeper counts as one) between you and the goal.

If you can do that, you're fine. If not, you will be called for offsides. Of course, just to make it a little more complicated, there are three exceptions:

1. If you're not involved in the play (in other words, you're off picking dandelions). It's only if you go for the ball or are passed the ball that being in the offside position matters; otherwise, the referee won't call it. Nonetheless, it's a good idea to try to be aware of where the defenders are because you're not doing your team much good if you can't be involved in the play. And one of your teammates might even pass you the ball not noticing that you're offside. Then you've given the other team a free kick.
2. If it's a throw-in, goal kick, or corner kick. You can't be offside on one of these.
3. If the other team kicks the ball to you. Obviously this would be accidental and lucky you, you wouldn't be called offside. But don't plan for it.

The penalty for offside is an indirect free kick for the other team. Look at the pictures on page 14 and mark which ones you think are offside.

For all the restarts—direct kicks, indirect kicks, throw-ins, corner kicks, and goal kicks—the referee will only blow the

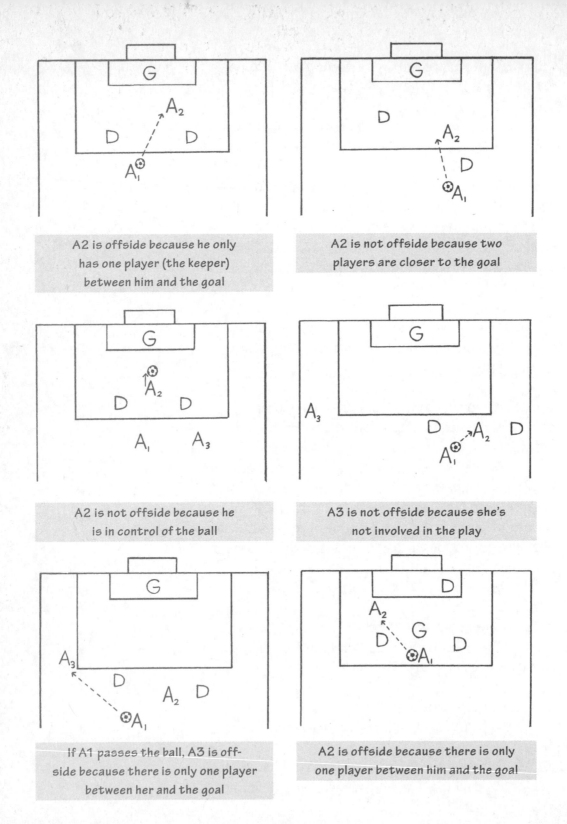

A2 is offside because he only has one player (the keeper) between him and the goal

A2 is not offside because two players are closer to the goal

A2 is not offside because he is in *control* of the ball

A3 is not offside because she's not involved in the play

If A1 passes the ball, A3 is offside because there is only one player between her and the goal

A2 is offside because there is only one player between him and the goal

whistle once, when the ball goes out-of-bounds or when a foul has been committed. Don't wait for another whistle telling you when to kick or throw. That's up to you. In fact, usually the faster you do it the better. Don't give the defense a chance to set up. The only time a referee will make you wait for a second whistle is when a team is subbing.

And that's basically the rules and regulations in a nutshell. Now you just need to find out where soccer got its crazy name and then you're ready to learn some moves.

WORDS to KNOW

FIFA: The Fédération Internationale de Football Association is the official soccer organization for world play. If a rule change is made, it's made by FIFA.

What's in a Name?

You might have heard that soccer is referred to as "football" in other languages. In which case, you're probably wondering why people in the United States call it "soccer." Where in the world did we get that name?

In England, during the early 1800s, there were two kinds of football games. One of them was called rugby football and the other was called association football because it was played by the rules set by FIFA, the Fédération Internationale de Football Association. Because association football was such a long name, people started calling it "assoc football" for short. That quickly turned into "soccer."

The word "soccer" in sign language

FUN FACT

Nicknames

One of the world's premiere women players and the 2006 FIFA player of the year is a Brazilian who is known to the soccer world only as Marta. Her full name is Marta Vieira da Silva, but in Brazilian tradition, only her first name goes on the back of her shirt. Even though Marta is the star of the team, take a look at the shirts of Marta's teammates on the Brazilian national team. They're all using only their first names, too. And it's not just a women's tradition. You may have heard of other one-named Brazilian soccer players: Pele, Ronaldo, and Ronaldinho.

At the same time, American football was becoming popular. So people in the United States found it pretty handy to say "soccer" instead of association football. It kept things a little clearer. In England, however, the opposite happened. Rugby football was shortened to just rugby, and so association football became just plain old "football." The assoc or soccer name was just dropped. The rest of the world didn't have the two-sport confusion, and they just called the sport football. It looks a little different in each language, but it's still the same game.

Here are the words for "soccer" in other languages:

◆ *Futbol* in Spanish
◆ *Voetbal* in Dutch (Holland)
◆ *Fussball* in German
◆ *Fotboll* in Swedish
◆ *Calcio* or *Futbol* in Italian
◆ *Aqsaqtuk* in Eskimo

Monkey in the Middle

If you have three people, try a good old-fashioned game of Monkey in the Middle. Two of you team up and try to keep possession of the ball while passing it back and forth. The third person does her best to get it away from you.

WORDS to KNOW

Dribbling: A series of short, crisp taps on the ball that allows the soccer player to run with the ball under his or her control.

occer is all about control. The team that controls the ball controls the game. Think about it. If you never let the other team have the ball, how can they score? Of course, that's completely unrealistic, but you can still try, right?

Knowing that you need to control the ball and actually getting it under control are two different things entirely. How do you get that big bouncing ball to behave? Take a look at some of the tips in this chapter and then get out and practice, practice, practice!

Feet First

Let's start with the feet, since the feet are used more than anything else to control the ball. And while you're starting simply, let's just have the ball sitting quietly in front of you, too. You don't need it to go bouncing around quite yet. You can move the ball forward, sideways, and backward just by giving it a short hard tap. When you do this while you're running, it's called dribbling, and it will be covered in great detail in Chapter 4.

But it's not often that the ball is just sitting there quietly waiting for you to move it. Usually it's in motion. Let's say it's rolling along the ground toward you. Your goal is to stop the ball so you can direct it the way you want it to go. So how do you do that? First, imagine the ball hitting a wall. It would bounce away from the wall, right? Now imagine the ball hitting a big squishy pillow. It would sink into the pillow and stop right there. Somehow you need to turn your foot into a big squishy pillow. It's not as hard as it sounds.

To begin, lift your foot up a few inches off the ground, about halfway up the soccer ball.

Then at the instant the ball meets your foot, drop your foot back just a little. In other words, let the ball push your foot

The foot is halfway up the
soccer ball for a trap

back when it makes contact. This allows the ball to "sink into" your foot the way it would sink into a pillow.

You and a friend should pass the ball back and forth to each other until you perfect this motion. It's one of the foundations of soccer, and it should be something you do without even thinking.

Now let's make it trickier. What do you do when the ball is in the air? Let's say it's a big lofted ball heading down to the ground right in front of you. How are you going to get control of it? The concept is the same. Hold your foot out and up in the air so that the ball will land on it. Then, just as the ball hits your foot, drop your foot down and let the ball "sink in."

When you're taking the ball out of the air, be careful not to lose your balance. You'll be standing on one leg as you raise the other, so make sure that leg is steady and strong. Bend the knee slightly and don't forget even though you can't use your arms to touch the ball, you can certainly hold them out to help steady your body.

Tip

Think of the ball as an egg or a water balloon that you don't want to break. That might help you treat it more gently.

Trapping the ball out of the air

Skill Master

This is two puzzles in one! First, get the soccer ball through the maze from START to GOAL. While you're doing that, carefully study the field full of practice players. Try to remember everything you see. Then turn to page 22 and answer the questions without looking back at the picture!

START

GOAL!

Again, the more you practice this, the better. You and a friend should now pick the ball up and toss it back and forth. Change the height of the tosses. If you are by yourself, you can still practice. Toss the ball into the air and "catch" it with your foot before it hits the ground.

Body Parts

Do you think soccer is a game played just with your feet? Think again! Sometimes the ball is bouncing up and down or flying through the air, and your feet are pretty worthless then. Instead you can use other body parts to control the ball. Circle the parts of the body that you think soccer players can use to control the ball:

Feet	Hands	Stomach
Chest	Head	Thighs
Elbows	Knees	
Fist	Shoulders	

If you circled feet, chest, head, stomach, and thighs, you're right! You definitely don't want to use anything that's part of your arms! It's off-limits from shoulders to fingertips. The knees were the tricky item in the list. It's not against the rules to use your knees, but it is certainly not a good idea if you're trying to control the ball.

Thighs

Some of the time when a ball is coming toward you a foot or two off the ground, you'll want to try to raise your foot high and get it under control with your foot. But sometimes that's just too awkward or the ball is too high. You need to use your thigh to control the ball.

FUN FACT

Ball Trap!

Many players try to trap the ball between the ground and the bottom of their cleats. In other words, they basically step on the ball. The upside of this trap is that the ball stops dead when you do it right. The downside is that it's really hard to do it right. Players end up stepping too hard, twisting their ankle, or missing the ball entirely. Until you're really good at soccer, leave this fancy move for the pros.

Tip

Get comfortable using body parts other than your foot. If you raise your foot too high and get it near someone's head, then the referee may call you for "dangerous play."

Skill Master Questions

1. How many players are on the field?
2. How many soccer balls are on the field?
3. What pattern does the goalie have on her shirt?
4. There is a player with her hair in a long braid. Where is she on the field?

BONUS: There are two players wearing the same uniform. What are their numbers?

Tip

By putting your arms out, you not only give yourself balance, but you also keep your arms and your hands out of the way of the ball so you aren't called for a handball.

When you're trapping with your thigh, make sure you're facing the ball. Then it's really the same concept as the foot, just a few feet higher. Raise your leg in the air and then as soon as the ball hits your thigh, drop it away.

Chest and Body

Now let's go up a little higher. There are two ways to control the ball with your chest and your body. One is to apply the same principles that you learned for the feet and the thighs. "Catch" the ball with your body by immediately giving a little to cushion the ball when it hits. If you're doing it this way, you'll want to lean back, with your arms out at your sides to give you balance. After you "catch" the ball, then lean forward and drop the ball at your feet. This method is good if you need to have the ball tightly controlled in a small area.

The second way to control a ball coming at chest level is to run through it; in other words, run right into it and keep running. This is the opposite of the "squishy pillow" theory. First,

Trapping the ball
with the chest

your body is generally soft enough that it won't bounce too far away. Second, if you are "running through it," you will be moving forward with the ball, so you don't have to worry about it getting away from you.

Use your body like a big wall this time—in other words, *don't* cushion the impact—and if you hit it square on, then it should bounce off straight in front of you. This is a good method to use if there's a little bit of space in front of you. Don't do it with defense around, because another player can snatch that ball up as soon as it bounces off you.

Head Games

And now finally we get to the head. Heading is a big part of soccer, but it's generally not recommended for anyone under the age of 12. Nonetheless, once you reach that age, you're going to have to start working on your head skills. Because the ball is in the air a lot, heading is a huge part of the game, and you'll be at a big disadvantage if you have to wait for the ball to come down. So here is a quick overview.

There are three basic rules you should follow for heading the ball. Concentrate on these three things no matter what type of ball you're trying to head, and you'll be successful:

1. Hit the ball square in the middle of your forehead. Face balls hurt and scalp balls don't go anywhere but straight up. (They hurt also.)
2. Meet the ball. In other words, you hit the ball instead of the ball hitting you.
3. Keep your eyes open and watch the ball all the way into your head.

Running through the ball

Warning!

Children under the age of 12 should not be heading the ball. Their bodies are still growing and aren't able to cope with the repeated blows to the head that come with heading the ball. The best advice is to wait until you're 12, keep practice to a minimum, and stop immediately if you feel any pain.

Once you master the well-headed ball, here are a few things you can do with that perfect header:

1. **Trapping header:** Run through the ball. You're trying to get the ball out of the air and under your control. Hit the ball square in the middle of your forehead, as you point your face down to the ground.
2. **Defensive header:** In this case you want to get the ball as far away from your goal as possible. Arch your back, get your arms out for balance, and then snap forward at the last minute, meeting the ball square in the middle of your forehead.
3. **Shooting or passing header:** This is similar to a defensive header in force, but you may also want to direct it to one side or the other by hitting it not-so-square on the forehead. Remember that the keeper can use his or her hands, so you can't wait for the ball to drop to your feet.
4. **Diving header:** Only do this in front of the goal. And if you're not good with pain, don't try it at all. If there's a low ball in front of the goal that you think you can dive at and get your head on, go for it. Throw your arms out in front of you and dive toward the ball, meeting it with your forehead. After you hit the ground, get up immediately so your head isn't kicked by all the feet around the goal area.

FUN FACT

Just a Kid

At the age of 14, Freddy Adu became the youngest person to ever play for a professional sports team in the United States. He was signed by the DC United. Not surprisingly, he also became the youngest person to ever score a goal for MLS, which he also did at age 14.

Diving header

The final thing you need to know about heading the ball is that timing is everything. And like everything else, that's only going to come with practice. But unless you're a good foot taller than everyone else, most of your headers are going to come off of jumps. You need to time your jump just perfectly to beat your opponent to the ball.

That's easy, right? Perfect timing and perfect control on every touch. If you can do that, look out soccer world! There's a superstar coming up.

Juggling

Now that you've learned to control the ball with every part of your body, you can start juggling. Juggling is one of the best ways you can practice good ball control. If you're picturing six flaming torches in the air at once, don't worry. Soccer juggling is a little different. It's only one ball. But you still need to keep it in the air. Sounds much easier, right? So don't be intimidated at the thought of it.

Start by dropping the ball onto your foot or thigh. Then use both feet and both thighs to keep the ball in the air. Not only will you become quickly familiar with how the ball bounces, but it will also give you a great sense of how increased force makes the ball bounce away, while less force makes it drop in front of you. Understanding this concept is the key to ball control.

Remember that soccer is a "no-hands" game, though, so once you get comfortable with the art of juggling a soccer ball, you should start with the ball on the ground instead of picking it up with your hands. The best way to get it up in the air with your foot is to step on the top of the ball, roll it back toward you, and scoop your foot underneath, popping the ball up in the air.

WORDS to KNOW

Juggling: Keeping the ball from touching the ground using your feet and thighs and even your head to pop the ball back up into the air.

Speed Drill

How should a pass receiver be? This tiny picture puzzle shows how!

Here are a few juggling games to play:

1. *For one person:* Start by dropping the ball on your foot or thigh. Count how many times you can put the ball back up in the air without it touching the ground. Try to beat your own record.

2. *For two or more people:* If you each have a ball, see who can keep it up in the air longest. If you have only one ball, work together to try to beat your own juggling records.

3. *For three or more people with only one ball:* The group should stand in a fairly small circle. One person begins with the ball. He tosses to someone else in the circle. That person juggles the ball as long as she wants (it might be only once) and then sends it to another person in the circle using her foot or thigh or possibly head to do so. This continues until the ball hits the ground. The person who was juggling at the time is eliminated. If the ball was being passed from one person to another, then the group decides whether the ball hitting the ground is the fault of the receiver or the sender. The winner is the last one left.

4. *For three or more people with lots of balls:* All players except one have a ball. They begin juggling them. The one without the ball is the "hunter." He moves among the players waiting for a ball to drop. If one does, he goes after it, trying to gain control. And that's with feet only, by the way! If he gains control, then he gets to juggle and the person who lost it becomes the hunter. If the juggler manages to get control, he continues juggling. If you want to have a winner in this game, then you can have the original hunter remain as a hunter with the new hunter. The last one left is the winner.

The First Touch

If you have time, you'll always want to get the ball under control first, before you begin dribbling or passing. But sometimes a defender is heading right for you. Then what? Remember reading about "running through" the ball when you're controlling it with your body? When you do that you are directing the ball with your body right from the start. In other words, right at the *first touch*. Instead of dropping the ball at your feet, you're sending it forward. When you get to be a more experienced soccer player, you should practice this first-touch philosophy with every ball you get, whether it's with your feet, thigh, body, or head.

Directing the ball on your first touch can sometimes make all the difference when you're trying to get away from a defender. Notice where the defenders are and use a quick second before the ball gets to you to think about where you'd like to put it. Sometimes it might be right in front of your feet, but other times you might want to send it in a certain direction.

Catch!

Get together with a friend and pass the ball back and forth. It's like playing catch, but with a soccer ball! Start by using two touches: you'll "catch" the ball first and then pass it. Once you feel comfortable with that, you can graduate to one-touch passing. See how many times the ball can go back and forth accurately.

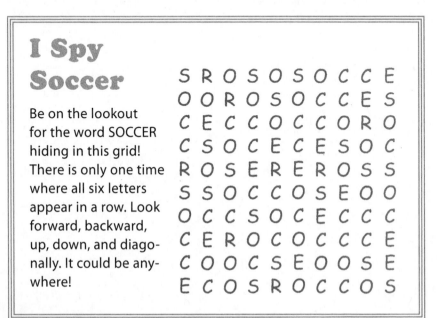

I Spy Soccer

Be on the lookout for the word SOCCER hiding in this grid! There is only one time where all six letters appear in a row. Look forward, backward, up, down, and diagonally. It could be anywhere!

```
S R O S O S O C C E
O O R O S O C C E S
C E C C O C C O R O
C S O C E C E S O C
R O S E R E R O S S
S S O C C O S E O O
O C C S O C E C C C
C E R O C O C C C E
C O O C S E O O S E
E C O S R O C C O S
```

JOKIN' AROUND

A not-so-smart fan arrives at a soccer game partway through the second half.

"What's the score?" he asks his friend as he settles into his seat.

"Zero to zero," comes the reply.

"And what was the score at halftime?" he asks.

In that case, you don't want your foot to be quite as cushiony. You'll want your foot to be a wall that the ball rebounds off instead. Position your foot so the rebound will be in the direction you want. Then as soon as the ball hits your foot, take off in that direction. You'll have the element of surprise in your favor and it might put you a step ahead.

That said, don't worry about directing the ball on the first touch until you've completely mastered the art of controlling the ball. You need to develop a soft touch before you increase the resistance and make a harder touch that pushes the ball in a certain direction.

CHAPTER 3
Power and Finesse

An announcer shouting GOOOOAAAALLLL!!!!!!!! A player ripping his shirt off in celebration. The drama of a shootout. Getting that elusive goal in soccer provides a thrill like no other. In basketball, you can score over 100 points in a game. Football games tend to be something like 26–20. Even baseball games, which usually have low scores, frequently end up with something like 6–5. But soccer is different. A 1–0 win is not uncommon, so the rare goal is extraordinarily sweet.

This chapter is going to show you all the skills you'll need to experience that sweet feeling yourself. You'll also learn how to pass the ball around the field, since most of the same skills are used whether you're shooting the ball or passing the ball. In the last chapter, you learned how to control the ball when it comes to you. In this one, you will learn how to get rid of it.

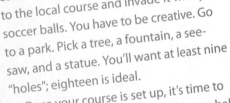

Soccer Golf

To play soccer golf, you first need a "golf" course. That doesn't mean you rush over to the local course and invade it with your soccer balls. You have to be creative. Go to a park. Pick a tree, a fountain, a see-saw, and a statue. You'll want at least nine "holes"; eighteen is ideal.

Once your course is set up, it's time to play. Each player should have a soccer ball. It's also handy to have a pencil and a piece of paper to keep score unless you have a really good memory. The first player "tees off" by kicking the soccer ball toward the goal. Then the next player goes. Count how many kicks it takes to hit the hole. Write that down as your score for that hole. At the end of your course, the player with the lowest score is the winner.

Perfect Passing

Soccer is a team sport, so it makes sense that sharing the ball among all your teammates is probably the best way to play. This sharing is called passing, and it's also the best way to move the ball toward the goal. Think of the other options.

- ◆ You could boot the ball halfway down the field. That would get the ball there faster, but who knows which team would end up with it.
- ◆ You could bring the ball down the field all by yourself. That would ensure that the ball stays in your possession, but it would take forever. And unless you're really skilled, there's a good chance that someone would steal it away from you.

So your best bet is to use a series of passes. There are several different kinds of passes, but they all have a few things in common:

♦ The first step in the pass, called a *plant*, is made with your nonkicking foot. This allows you to shift your weight as you are making your pass, which will give the pass more power.
♦ Your planting foot must always be pointed in the direction you want the ball to go.
♦ The pass must be crisp. A lazy slow roller is going to be intercepted in a second.
♦ The pass must be accurate. If you don't get the ball to your teammate, it's likely to go to the opponents.
♦ The pass should lead your teammate. Don't pass it to where she is now. Think of where she'll be in the next two seconds. Pass it a few feet in front of her, so she can keep running at the same pace.

Keep all these ideas in mind as you learn about the different types of passes.

The Short Pass

Many times your passes will be short, about 10 yards or less. For this pass, your best bet is to use the inside of your foot. This is called a *push pass*. Take a step toward the ball with your nonkicking foot, and plant that foot next to the ball, about 6 inches away. Your weight should be on this foot, which lets your other leg swing freely. As your body moves forward with this plant, turn your kicking foot sideways and lock it in an L-shaped position with your leg. If you think about turning your foot and leg into a hockey stick, it might help you to better picture what the push pass looks like. All the swing comes

Speed Drill

This tiny picture puzzle shows the important first step of any pass. What is it?

WORDS to KNOW

Plant: A step toward the ball that shifts your weight forward and gives you more power for your kick.

Push pass: A short, accurate pass using the inside of the foot.

Follow through: A term used in many sports. It means that the swinging motion doesn't stop with impact. The leg (or baseball bat or tennis racket) continues to move forward in the same direction.

FUN FACT

Outside-of-the-Foot Pass

You can also use the outside of your foot to make a pass, but it will likely be no more than a nudge. You won't get much power using this part of the foot, but if your teammate is near enough it might allow you to play a little "keep away" with a defender.

Hot Potato

A good game to play using your short ball-passing skills is Hot Potato. You'll probably need at least four players, one ball, and a timer. Set the timer and start passing the ball around your circle. Whoever ends up with the ball when the timer goes off is out. Another way to play is that, instead of being out, she gets a letter in the word POTATO each time she's caught with the ball. In other words, the first time she gets a P, the second time an O, and so on. That way, it takes six turns to be eliminated. This game is great for working on your accuracy and your speed in passing.

from your hips, not from your knee joint.

Now hit the ball squarely in the middle. If you hit it on the top of the ball, you'll lose much of your power. If you hit it low on the ball, it will pop up a little and have some backspin, which will cost you some distance.

You should already have your planting foot pointing in the direction you want the ball to go, and now

The foot is halfway up the soccer ball for a trap

you should follow through with your kicking foot in that same direction. Make sure you kick the ball hard enough to make it move quickly—no lazy little rollers that can be snagged by the defense. However, you also don't want to kick it so hard that it's difficult for your teammate to control. Lots of practice will help you develop the right touch.

The push pass is the most accurate pass. This is mostly because you use such a large part of your shoe to move the ball. It's hard not to hit it exactly where you want it because so much of your foot is involved. As long as you follow through to your target, the ball will go where you want it to go.

The Long Pass

Many times in a soccer game, you'll see a teammate down the field who is wide open. A push pass isn't going to cut it. Now you're going to need the *instep pass*. You might want to think of it as the shoelace pass, because that's exactly the part of the foot you're going to use to kick it.

The instep pass is key for any soccer player. This is a much more powerful pass than the push

pass, and it also lets you loft the ball into the air if you need to. Both of these come in pretty handy if you're trying to get the ball downfield quickly.

Many young players get in the bad habit of using their toe to kick a long ball, because early on that might give them a longer kick. Don't make this mistake. The toe kick will never be as accurate. Always practice proper technique right from the start, and eventually you'll be able to achieve the same distance.

To kick the ball with your instep, you'll want to plant your foot in the same place as the push pass, about 2 or 3 inches out from the ball. In the instep pass, however, you're probably going to plant with more of a hop than a step.

Now, instead of holding your leg rigid, like a hockey stick, get your knee into the action. As you hop forward, your kicking leg swings backward, bending at the knee. Then, as soon as you plant, swing the leg forward, snapping both the knee joint and the hip joint forward. Keep your toe pointed down and whack the ball with your instep. Try to hit the ball in the center; if you hit it a little off to the side, it will spin.

WORDS to KNOW

Instep pass: a powerful pass that lets the player loft the ball into the air by striking it with her instep.

Instep: The arched middle portion of the foot located directly in front of the ankle and under the shoelaces.

FUN FACT

The Soccer-Style Kick

Many beginning players use their toes to kick the ball because it gives them more distance than the instep. This is a mistake. If you practice the instep pass, it won't take you long until it's just as powerful as the toe-poke, and it's certainly a whole lot more accurate, as a Hungarian football player named Pete Gogolak showed the NFL. Until he came along, the field goal kickers were kicking with their toes. Coming from Hungary, Pete had played soccer, so his long kicks were all soccer style. He was so successful that now, a soccer-style instep kick is all you see—in *both* soccer and football.

The instep pass

Fast Pass

Use your instep to start the ball driving down the field to a teammate. Continue alternating foot to ball until the path reaches the goal at the other end of the field. You can move up and down, or side to side, but not diagonally. If you hit a player's hand, a foul is called and you have to start again!

Extra skill play: Using just your finger to trace the path, see how long it takes you to do this puzzle. Try again in 10 minutes and see if it takes you just as long. Try again ten minutes after that. What's your best time?

START

GOAL!

Keep your knee over the ball, which will keep the ball on the ground.

There are times, however, when you want that ball up in the air. You'll use the instep pass for this—not the toes!—but your approach will be slightly different. Place your plant foot a good distance back from the ball, about 10 inches, rather than next to it. Then, lean back a little when you contact the ball. Remember, if your knee is over the ball, the ball will stay on the ground. If you have your knee back from the ball, the ball will rise into the air. Also, try to contact the ball on its lower half. This will also help lift it.

The pass on the ground is easier for your teammates to control, but there are times when the lofted pass comes in handy. It's used mainly to get over the heads of defenders. If you see a player who is wide open across the field, you can loft the ball over to her, bypassing the defenders. A lofted pass

is also used for shots on goal and free kicks—such as corner kicks, goal kicks, direct kicks, and indirect kicks—when defenders set up to block everything on the ground.

Thinking Backward

Passing backward is a great strategic move. If you're having trouble moving the ball forward, back up and try again. Maybe a different route will work. It's better to take a little longer and hold on to the ball than to push it up quickly and lose possession. You should think of soccer as a game of keep away. The longer you keep possession, the more chance you have of winning. If the safest pass is backward, then go for it!

Passing Strategy

Now take this short true-false quiz to find out what you know about passing strategy.

1. If the ball has spent a long time on one side of the field, it's a good idea to switch it to the other side.
2. It's always better to pass than to dribble.
3. A pass is an easy way to get around a defender.
4. The only lofted passes are long balls.

And now here are the answers. Let's see how you did.

1. *True.* If a ball has been on one side of the field for a long time, there's a good chance that the defense has shifted to that side. Everyone wants to be part of the action, so you might find the other team drifting over toward the play. If you can switch the ball to the other side of

Get in the Action

Now that you've learned all the different passes, it's time to play a game. You and your friends should find a field somewhere and split up into two equal teams. You use one ball, but you don't need any goals. To get a point, a team has to get six passes in a row, without the other team touching the ball. Set a limit such as five points or twenty minutes of play, so that you know when the game is over.

Tip

Many soccer players find it easier to lift the ball if they approach it from an angle.

35

WORDS to KNOW

Give-and-go pass: Also called the wall pass, it is a way of getting around a defender by "bouncing" the ball off one of your teammates. Your teammate receives the ball while you run around the defender and then passes it back to you when you're free.

Chip: A sharp, stabbing kick that gives the ball some air and backspin but doesn't give much distance, so the player is able to loft the ball over an opponent's head without the ball going too far.

The give-and-go pass

the field, with a long lofted pass, for instance, then you might find a teammate who has no one guarding him.

2. *False.* If no one is moving in to defend against you, you might want to take a few dribbles, especially if no one is open for a pass. If you are unguarded, then that means ten of the other team's players are guarding only nine of yours. That's not the best situation to start passing the ball. Take what they'll give you. If they'll let you dribble all the way to the goal, then take a shot, too. Don't forget, though, once they do commit to defending you, you need to get rid of the ball quickly. Look to pass it off to the person who was left open by that move.

3. *True.* If you see a wide-open field in front of you with only one defender between you and the goal, then a *give-and-go pass* is the perfect thing to use. Pass the ball to a nearby teammate and sprint forward around the defender. The defender will most likely turn toward your pass, and if your teammate is paying attention, she now has the opportunity to pass the ball back to you while you're unguarded for a moment. That's the essence of the give-and-go. That's why it's also called a wall pass. Your teammate has acted like a wall that you can bounce the ball off, then receive it, and go on.

4. *False.* Occasionally you might want to loft the ball over the opponent's head without it going too far. This is called a *chip.* Essentially you want to use the same motion as a lofted pass, getting your instep under the ball and leaning backward, but you don't want to follow through. Make your kick a sharp stab at the ball rather than a smooth kick. This should give it some air and some backspin but not much distance.

Shooting Skills

A ball lofted into the upper right-corner goal. A bullet drilled to the far left of the keeper. A diving header off a corner kick. A nudge with the outside of the foot, catching the keeper out of position. A dribbler rolling past the goalkeeper's fingertips. All of these are goals; all are equal no matter how spectacular or unspectacular they look, and all will make you a hero with your teammates. Officially, a shot counts as a goal when the ball crosses fully over the goal line and in between the two goalposts.

Most of your hard shots will be taken with your instep. This will give you the most powerful kick. When you're passing, you have to be worried about sending the ball to your teammate at a speed he can handle. When you're shooting, the last thing you want is for the goalkeeper to be able to handle it.

Sometimes placement is more important than power. If you're close to the goal, you're going to want to use the inside of your foot to make a very accurate, perfectly placed finesse shot. You want don't want to wind up and boot a ball that

Double Jeopardy

One good passing game for four players is called Double Jeopardy. Have two players line up on one line and two others stand across from them at a good passing distance for your level. Use two balls, one on each side. Now start passing the ball back and forth. The team who can get both balls on one side is the winner.

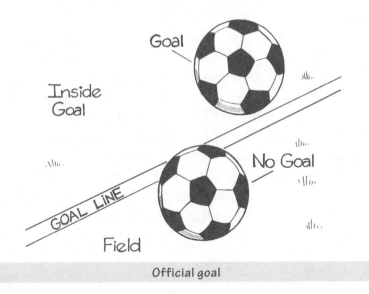

Goal

Inside Goal

No Goal

GOAL LINE

Field

Official goal

Teamwork

It takes two players to make a successful pass. And it takes two halves to make a successful compound word! Listed below are two sets of three-letter words. First unscramble the words in column A. Then, match each word in column A with a word in column B to form a new word. We've done the first one for you.

HINT: The word in column A should always come first.

A	B	
~~YEE~~	BID	EYELID
ORF	ROT	_____
NPA	AGE	_____
ONT	FIT	_____
RAC	TRY	_____
OTC	~~LID~~	_____
AMN	ICE	_____
UTO	TON	_____

might go straight to the keeper. Instead you want to direct the ball away from the keeper and into the goal.

The power shot and the finesse shot are the two most basic types of shots, but there are quite a few others, and they're a little trickier.

◆ **Header:** Players shouldn't be directing the ball with their heads until they are about 12 years old. But after that, using the head to take a shot can be very effective. Remember the keeper can reach up and use her hands to grab the ball. If you have to wait until the ball gets to foot level, you'll never connect in front of the goal. But if you jump up and direct that air ball with your forehead, you might just score.

◆ **Volley:** A volley is a shot where you connect with the ball while it's in the air. When you're in front of the goal, you're not going to be given much time to settle the ball in front of you, get control, and get off a nice, sweet shot. To kick a volley, you'll want to use your instep. Lean forward over the ball to keep it low, and keep your eye on the ball. Make sure you use your arms to keep your balance since you'll be taking the shot on one leg. Because the ball is coming toward you with some force already, this shot will be quite powerful.

◆ **Half-volley:** A shot in which the player kicks the ball immediately after it has bounced. The ball is still in the air but only a bit off the ground. The technique

to shoot a half-volley is very similar to that of the volley. Timing is everything.

◆ **Slider:** If the ball is near the goal line and just needs a nudge in the right direction, the slider shot might be your best bet. Slide into the ball, much as a baseball player would slide into home plate. Chances are there will be a defender right on that ball trying to get it out of there, so you need to make sure to get your foot on the ball, not on the defender. You have to touch the ball first or you'll be called for tripping.

Shooting Strategy

You can't get the ball into the goal if you don't take the shot. That may sound ridiculous because it's so obvious, but too many players goof around in front of the goal, waiting for the perfect shot. I've got news for you. It's not going to come. The defenders are not going to back off and let you line up and place your shot perfectly. Just get in there and shoot the ball. Of course, if a teammate does happen to be wide open go ahead and pass it, but don't do it just because he has a better kick or a stronger foot. If you find yourself within shooting distance of the goal, go for it.

Here is a top ten list for shooting tips:

1. **Use both feet.** You won't have time to set the ball up in front of your stronger foot, so be sure to practice with both your left and your right. In fact, you should practice with the weaker foot even more often than you practice with your dominant foot.

2. **Be aggressive.** The defense does not want to be called for a push inside the penalty box, so they might be reluctant to be too physical.

Knockout

Knockout is a great game to practice your shooting. It's especially good for practice volleys. Find a wall and mark off a goal area. You and your friends line up in a single line in front of it. The first person takes a shot at the goal. The next person must get the rebound and one-touch it back into the goal, and so on. When a person misses, he's knocked out. The last one left is the winner.

Player of the Year ... Again

It's not hard to argue the point that Landon Donovan is the best men's soccer player ever to come from the United States. He won the Honda Player of the year award four times (2002, 2003, 2004, and 2007), and became the youngest person ever to achieve 50 goals and 50 assists. He is also the all-time leading scorer for the U.S. National Team with 35 goals. Currently he plays for the Los Angeles Galaxy.

Practice That Shot

A good way to practice shooting for the sides of the goal is to place two cones about 3 feet in from each of the goalposts. Now play your regular soccer game, but the only goal that counts is the ball that goes between a cone and a goalpost. Anything that goes between the two cones is not a goal.

JOKIN' AROUND

Two friends get to the stadium just before a big game between the New York MetroStars and D.C. United. The first friend says, "I wish I'd brought our piano to the stadium."

"Why would you bring a piano to a soccer game?" asks the second friend.

"Because I left the tickets on it."

3. **Take balls out of the air.** Use the volley, half-volley, and headers whenever you have the opportunity.

4. **Don't kick it to the keeper.** This sounds obvious, but believe it or not, players tend to go for the middle of the goal, right where the goalkeeper is. Maybe that's because those brightly colored shirts just draw the eye right there.

5. **Aim for the four corners.** These are the four spots farthest away from the keeper. This is similar to the previous tip, but it really gets you to focus on location. Don't worry about missing the goal. This will happen time and again, but the payoff is huge if you can find a corner.

6. **Pay attention to the size of your goalkeeper.** If you're playing against a very short keeper in a regulation-size goal, then a lofted ball is going to be successful. If you're older and your opponent's keeper is almost the size of an adult, then send the ball low. It's going to be a lot harder for him to bend down or dive for a low ball than to stay standing up to block the high ball.

7. **Shoot for the far post.** If you're approaching the goal from the side, aim for the far top corner. The keeper will be trying to cut off the angle of your shot, and this area is vulnerable. Even if it doesn't go in, it might create an opportunity for one of your teammates.

8. **Don't wait for the perfect shot.** You just might be allowing the defense to make a perfect clear instead.

9. **Use the 18-yard line as a physical reminder that it's time to take a shot.**

10. **Follow your shot.** As soon as you take your shot, charge into the goal. Even if you end up kicking it straight to the keeper, there's a good chance that it will be too hard for her to handle on her first touch. Any sort of rebound from her hand, a defender, or the goalpost is another opportunity for you to put it in the goal.

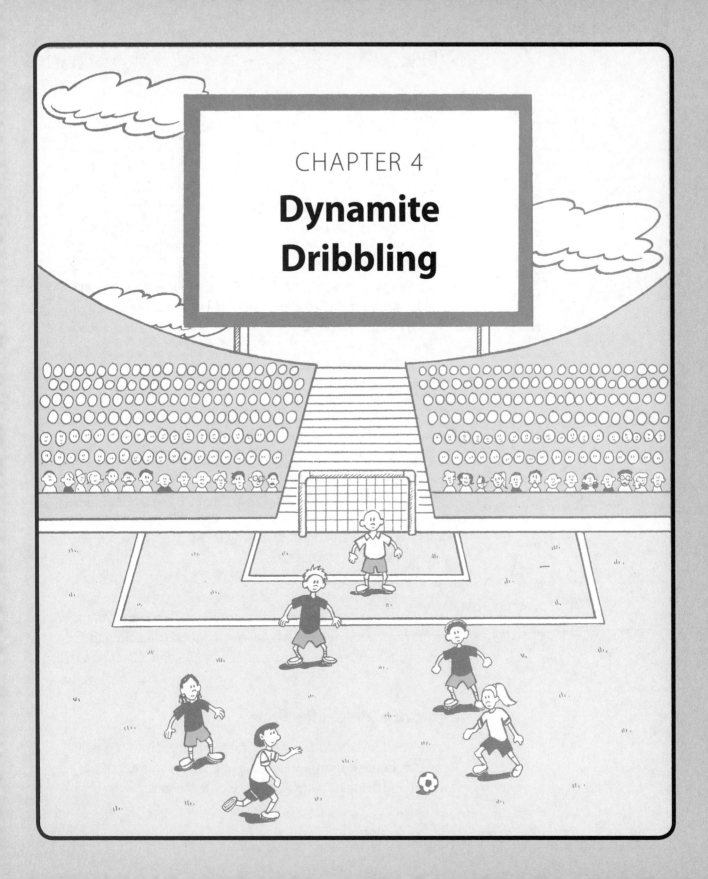

CHAPTER 4

Dynamite Dribbling

So there it is, a leather soccer ball, sitting in front of you. How do you get the ball rolling? A small, but sharp, tap with your foot will work just fine. Do it again and you've started dribbling. Dribbling is the way that soccer players move the ball up and down the field by themselves.

Can you guess how many parts of the foot soccer players use? If you guessed four, you're right! Soccer players use the insides of their feet, the outsides of their feet, the bottoms of their feet, and the insteps. But what about the toes, you ask? The toes are kind of like knees. It's legal to use them, but you won't get much control.

Start Simple

You can practice dribbling anywhere: on a field, in the park, your backyard, or even inside if you're allowed. To start, put the ball on the ground and move it forward. Try to get from one end of your playing area to the other. Be sure to use every part of both feet. The more ways you know how to dribble, the more options you have when you're trying to get away from a defender. Make a point of dribbling most often with the parts that don't feel as comfortable.

Practice dribbling whenever you get a chance. You don't need much space and you don't need anyone else to do it with you. The more chances your feet get to touch the ball, the more comfortable they will be when you're out on the field and the more you'll understand just which way the ball is going to roll.

Tip

The closer you keep the ball to your feet, the more control you'll have.

Practice Makes Perfect

Once you feel comfortable moving the ball around the field, you can make it more interesting and turn yourself into a whiz-bang dribbler by trying some of these variations:

1. Dribble only with your left foot and then only with your right. Then dribble alternating between the two feet every time.

2. Dribble only with the inside of your foot. Then dribble with only the outside. Then just use your instep. Try alternating between those three.

3. Make your course curvy instead of a straight line. Pretend that the trees and bushes are defenders that you have to avoid. Use sweatshirts or leaves or anything else if you're playing in a place without trees.

4. Place your hand under your eyes to block your vision of the ball. Now try to dribble through your course. The best players are able to look up and see what the field situation is like. They can't be watching the ball the whole time.

5. Time yourself. Set up a course and see how fast you can get through it. Don't do this in a wide-open field, however, because all you'll end up doing is kicking it much too far ahead. You want to practice speed in an area where you still need to control the ball and keep it close to your feet.

6. Use the line markings on the field. Dribble up to the 6-yard line, turn around and dribble back to the baseline. Now dribble to the 18, then back to the 6. Now go to the middle of the field, turn around, and go back to the 18.

7. Turn some of these dribbling exercises into a race.

Regular practice with your dribbling will make it become automatic, which is an important step in moving toward the fancy footwork of fakes. Think of it like math class. You have to learn basic addition, subtraction, and multiplication before you can learn algebra. You need the base in order to build.

A Soccer Spin on a Classic Game

Red Light, Green Light has always been a great kids' game, and it can be played with a soccer ball as well. One person is the "traffic light" at the far end of the field. The rest are the "cars." They each have a ball. The player at the far end yells, "Green light!" and turns around. The cars all begin dribbling their balls until they hear the traffic light yell, "Red light!" at which point they all must put a foot on the ball. If any players can't put their foot on the ball because it's too far away from them, then they're sent back to the beginning. The winner (and next traffic light) is the player who crosses the field first. This really teaches you to keep the ball close yet still dribble quickly.

Practice, Practice, Practice

First, read this advice from Michelle Akers, a U.S. Women's World Cup player. She says, "My suggestion is to use your [weaker foot] as much as possible. That means use it all the time, every time, for everything you do on the soccer field. Use it in warm-up, for dribbling, shooting, receiving, in drills, when you train extra, etc. Whatever you are doing, use only your [weak] foot."

Now, figure out where to put each of the scrambled letters in the following puzzle. They all fit in spaces under their own column. When you have filled in the grid, you will be able to see what Michelle Akers promises this practicing will help you do!

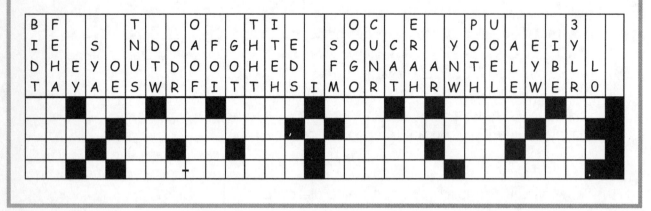

Fancy Footwork

Once you've mastered the straight dribble, it's time to add to your bag of tricks. And "tricks" is the right word! You want to use your dribbling to fool the defenders. There won't be many teams that will let you take the ball from one end of the field to the other without trying to stop you. So what can you do?

If a defender is closing in on you quickly, the first thing you're going to want to do is look to pass the ball off to someone who is open. But many times, you don't have that option, and it's all up to you. Uh oh. What now? Well, it's time for a fake.

There are many different fakes, but they generally fall into two categories: fakes that turn you in a new direction and fakes that allow you to keep going forward.

Changing directions works best when the defender is running alongside you, going in the same direction. That way her momentum will be carrying her forward and it will take her a

Tip

If a player isn't fooled by your turn, try another one immediately. So now you've turned 360 degrees, and you're heading right back in the direction you started.

second to recover and go in the other direction, especially if you catch her by surprise.

Many times your turn will redirect you back toward your own goal, but this isn't a problem. If the turn lets you escape from the defender, you're in good shape. Keeping the ball in your possession is the key to winning. And now you have a second or two to look up and find a teammate who is looking for a pass.

Here are some of the most popular turns:

◆ **The drag back:** This is where the bottom of your foot comes into play. You step on top of the ball and pull it back behind you. Spin 180 degrees and take off. When you turn around after doing a drag back, turn toward the leg that pulled the ball back. That way you see the ball the whole time you're turning.

The drag back

◆ **The inside turn:** Step over the ball and using the inside of your foot, push the ball back in the other direction.

The inside of the foot turn

◆ **The outside turn:** For this one, you'll want to nudge the ball backward with the outside of your foot, again turning your body 180 degrees and following the ball.

The outside of the foot turn

◆ **The box turn:** This is similar to the inside turn, but you push the ball under your body before you turn your body. Make an L-shape with your two feet and push the ball under your body. Then spin and take off in the other direction.

Try Turning

To see how well a turn works, you and a friend should try it without a ball. Find a good starting point, like a tree or a fence. The idea is to have a race, away from the tree and then back to it. But your friend isn't going to know how far out you plan to go. Say ready, set, go, and then you both start sprinting away from it in one direction. Suddenly, turn around and sprint back to the starting place. I'll bet you beat your friend. Now let her be the one who turns. This time, she'll beat you.

JOKIN' AROUND

Question: Why do soccer players have terrible table manners?
Answer: Because they're always dribbling.

Speed is the key to a great turn. With a speedy move, you catch the defender by surprise when you are both running quickly in the same direction. You know when you're going to make the turn, so your body is prepared to slow down and go the other way. But the defender has no idea. He is going to need an extra second to do all that, and that's when you lose him. However, if you don't move quickly leading up to the turn, then the defender will find it much easier to stop and turn with you. Or if you don't make your turn quickly, then he'll find it easy to catch up with you afterward.

But what if the defender is coming full speed right at you? Turning and running in the opposite direction might sound really appealing, but it's not your best option. The defender will actually have an advantage! This is the time for a fake.

Fake Basics

A fake basically means that you're going to try to make the opponent think that you're going in one direction when you really plan to move in the other direction. Time for some superior acting skills!

There are a whole bunch of different fakes, but all of them have a few things in common. You have to:

◆ Be fast
◆ Use your whole body
◆ Be convincing
◆ Stay low

No matter what fake you try, you aren't going to fool anyone if you don't do those four things.

The first one is obvious. If you're trying to fake someone out, you have to make your move fast. If you take too long, then even if you do fool the other player at first, he's going to have plenty of time to recover.

The second tip is important, too. You might not realize it, but you generally move your whole body when you change directions or make a move. Many players give themselves away when they only fake with their legs. The defender can tell that you're really not going that way because it doesn't look natural. Or in other words, your fake looks fake. So make sure you get your whole body involved.

Third, be convincing. In general, this tip should follow naturally if you're concentrating on the first two tips. If you're moving quickly and using your whole body, you'll most likely look as though you're going the way you're faking. Just make sure that your fake is significant enough to be noticed. Make a dramatic hard shift to the left or right with your whole body, not just a slight lean.

And finally, stay low and keep your knees bent. It's going to be hard to keep your balance with all that shifting back and forth. You want to get the opponent off balance, not yourself.

Here are some common fakes:

◆ **The step-over:** Swing your leg as though you're going to pass or shoot the ball, but instead lift it a little higher and step over the ball. Then push the ball in the opposite direction with the outside of your foot.

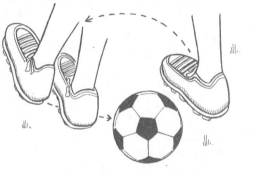

The step-over

FUN FACT

The Goal of the Century

In 2002, FIFA asked fans to vote for their favorite goal of the twentieth century. The winner was a goal made by Argentina's Diego Maradona in the 1986 World Cup tournament. He received the ball on his team's side of the field and then managed to dribble 60 meters, through five different defenders, take the shot, and score.

Practice Makes Perfect

You'll be able to practice a ton of shielding, turning, and faking if you play a little one-on-one with a friend. Set up two goals—they can be as simple as T-shirts on the ground that you have to hit—and then try to score.

- **The shimmy:** Shift your whole body in one direction without lifting your feet off the ground. Then kick the ball in the other direction.
- **The stop and start:** For this move, you want to dribble hard in one direction and then stop the ball as if you're going to switch directions. As soon as the defender moves to block you in your new direction, continue in the same direction.

Shielding

Sometimes the other team's defensive skills far outpace your dribbling skills. No amount of fancy footwork is going to get you past them. You're desperate to pass the ball, but no one's open. You know you have to protect the ball at all costs, but what can you do? It's easy. You put your body between the ball and the defender and continue dribbling, keeping the ball very close to your feet but as far away from the opponent as possible.

This is also called *shielding* the ball. You are acting like a protective shield placed between the defender and the ball.

It takes quite a bit of skill to shield the ball for a long time, so you really only choose this option when you have every intention of getting rid of the ball quickly. Look and listen for a teammate who has come to help you. As a last resort, you can also try to escape by making a strong fake move with your body in one direction. If the defender goes for it, then take off in the other direction.

Shielding the ball

WORDS to KNOW

Shielding: The process of keeping your body between the defender and the ball to prevent the defender from getting to the ball.

Tip

When you are shielding the ball from an opponent, remember your arms are off limits. Not only can't you use them to touch the ball, but you also can't use them to keep your opponent back. Use your body to block him from the ball. Don't hold out your arms.

Smart Moves

Now that you know all the great moves, you probably want to know some strategy. When are you supposed to dribble instead of passing or shooting? There are a few smart guidelines.

First of all, if you're all by yourself and no one is challenging you, go ahead and dribble. Take as much of the field as the defenders will give you. It's hard to imagine that any team would let you take the ball from one end of the field to the other, but until they send someone in to stop you, give it a try. However, just because you see a defender approaching doesn't mean that you should immediately pass the ball. Wait until he actually commits to challenging you. Otherwise you'll make it easy for him to intercept your pass.

When they do approach you, however, it's time to rethink. You could try to use a fake to get by a defender, but that doesn't have a high success ratio. If there's an open player nearby, you can send the ball to her. She can then pass it back to you for the easy give-and-go pass that you learned about in Chapter 3. This is a much better, almost foolproof, option than trying to dribble around the defender.

You also don't want to be dribbling when you're defending in front of your own goal. That's a really dangerous area to be fooling around in. Instead, get the ball out of there! Use a series of short passes or one long kick, but clear it out of the goal area. Don't rely on any fancy footwork because if you get burned, then you're risking a goal.

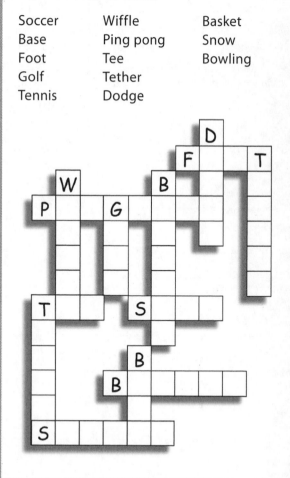

Keep Your Eye on the Ball

All thirteen of the words in this puzzle can be followed by the word BALL. See how many words you can figure out and fit into the criss-cross grid. **HINT:** We've left you the first letter of each!

Soccer	Wiffle	Basket
Base	Ping pong	Snow
Foot	Tee	Bowling
Golf	Tether	
Tennis	Dodge	

You might think that if you're in front of the other team's goal, the advice would be just the opposite, but that's not the case. You don't want to dribble there, either. This time, though, forget passing. Shoot! Dribble if you need to get clear to take a shot, but if you're inside that box, boot the ball into the goal.

So, to put it simply:

Goal areas = No dribbling

Finally, you don't want to dribble if there's someone else wide open and closer to the goal. Even if you're a fast runner, you're not going to be faster than a good hard pass. So send the ball down the field to your teammate and race to support her. The key to remember in this situation is that your teammate has to be "wide open." Just because your teammate is closer to the goal doesn't mean that she's able to receive a pass. This is especially true if no one is guarding you. Think about it. If no one is on you, the other team has ten of their players guarding the other nine players on your team. You might just want to keep the ball and start tap, tap, tapping your way toward the goal.

CHAPTER 5

In the Net

oalkeeper, keeper, goaltender, goalie, handman, net-minder—there are tons of different names for the person who stands in front of the big net known as the goal (lunatic is another). And that player has even more responsibilities than he or she has names. He's the last line of defense when the opponents are on the attack, and he's the first offensive effort when his team gains possession.

The Nitty-Gritty

The goalkeeper is so important that the position is set apart from the rest of the positions in three ways:

1. The goalkeeper wears a different uniform.
2. She gets to touch the ball with her hands.
3. She gets her own chapter in this book.

Fancy Clothes

The goalkeeper has the greatest uniform—it doesn't have to match anything. In fact, it is required to be a different color from the shirts of the field players on both teams. Sometimes, it's just a bright color, but many keepers today love to wear something a little wilder, with swirls or tie-dye designs or even a bull's-eye.

There are three reasons behind the keeper's wild shirt:

1. The first and most important reason is that the referee has to be able to distinguish between a regular field player and the keeper. The ref must know in an instant whether the person touching the ball with his hand is the one who is allowed to do so.

Elbow Protection

Most keeper shirts are long-sleeved because it allows them to have some padding in the elbow.

2. Second, the wilder the shirt, the less likely it is to match the shirts of the other team. If a player just has a royal blue jersey, for instance, she'll have to come up with a different shirt when her team plays a team whose shirts are royal blue.

3. The last reason doesn't have anything to do with the rules, but it has a lot to do with a player's brain. Studies have shown that players focus on the keeper's bright shirt and tend to kick it right to him. The mass of color in the center of the goal just attracts their eyes. That's why the more outrageous the shirt is, the better.

A goalie shirt to draw on

Because the goalkeeper can't rely on everyone kicking the ball to her just because she's wearing a wild shirt, she also has to rely on her ability to catch or stop the ball from going into the goal. Helping her do this is a pair of keeper gloves. Almost all goalkeepers above a certain level wear gloves. Gloves give the keeper a much better grip on the ball. Some are simple gloves with a piece of rubber sewn into the palm and finger areas, but some are way more elaborate with finger guards to both strengthen and protect a keeper's hands.

The rest of the outfit isn't as important. Many keepers like to wear padded shorts. These shorts have cushions in the hip area, so if the keeper has to dive to save the ball, it won't hurt so much when he hits the ground. And just like every other player, the keeper wears cleats, socks, and shin guards.

FUN FACT

Not Slippery When Wet

You might see goalkeepers wetting down or even spitting on their gloves. Though it seems like water might make a glove more slippery, the opposite is true. The rubber on the gloves gets much stickier when wet.

Uniform Uniforms

Oops—goalies are supposed to wear shirts that are different from the rest of the team. These goalies look too much the same! Cross out the three pairs of goalies who are wearing exactly the same shirts. Circle the one goalie who has a shirt that is different from everyone else's. This goalie will get to play today!

Extra Rules for Hands and Feet

Now that the keeper is dressed to kill—or at least block, stop, and save—it's time to get in the goal and learn about the extra rules that are designed to help (and limit!) the keeper's ability to stop the ball.

In front of the goal, there are two boxes. A small one extends 6 feet out from the goal, and a larger one goes out 18 feet from the goal.

The first box is irrelevant to the keeper, but the second marks the boundaries for hand use. Inside the box, the keeper can use her hands. Outside the box, she can't.

Now just because there is a box with boundaries, it doesn't mean that the keeper is limited to that space. She's allowed to come out of that box whenever she wants. She can even run down to the other end and score a goal. She just has to remember that leaving the box turns her into a field player, and she can only use her feet. But most keepers choose not to leave their box, because they lose a huge advantage when they can't use their hands.

There's one other time that a keeper is required to resort to her feet. If a teammate is in trouble and can't find a field player to pass to, he can pass the ball back to the keeper. In this instance, however, the keeper essentially becomes a field player, and she's not allowed to pick the ball up with her hands.

There are two exceptions to this rule:

◆ If the teammate uses another part of the body besides the foot to pass back, a keeper may use her hands. More often than not, the ball is headed back to the keeper in this scenario.

◆ If the teammate has miskicked the ball and it ends up going unintentionally to the keeper, then it is also okay for the keeper to use her hands to pick it up.

A few decades ago, passing back to the keeper was perfectly acceptable, but players were using this option so often that it slowed the game down and made it a little boring for the spectators. Forcing the keeper to use her feet on a pass back has reduced this play considerably. In fact, passing back to the keeper can now be quite risky at younger levels of play. As defenders and keepers become more comfortable with each other and as their skills improve, passing back to the keeper can be a smart way to restart the whole play and allow the defense to settle. The keeper just has to remember the rules.

Regardless of how the ball gets to the keeper, one of the other goalkeeper rules is a time limit on the release. Once the keeper has the ball in her hands, she has six seconds to get rid of it. Most keepers like to run to the front of the box before throwing or kicking the ball to their teammates because it allows them to gain a little more ground. But they need to do it quickly. If the keeper takes longer than six seconds, the other team gets an indirect kick.

And finally, once the goalkeeper has released the ball, she cannot touch it again until someone else has touched it.

Tip

Just because you have six seconds to release the ball, you don't have to use it all. When you catch the ball, quickly scan the field. Is there anyone who might be totally free or breaking away from the defense? If so, you want to get the ball to that player quickly!

FUN FACT

Full Attack

If a team is losing by one goal late in the game, the coach may pull the goalkeeper out of the goal to act as an eleventh field player. Although the team takes the risk of leaving the goal wide open, they're already down and losing by one or two isn't going to make any difference. By adding an extra field player, however, they might be able to overwhelm the defense and score the tying goal.

Catch and Release

You've been catching a variety of balls since you were in preschool, so you probably think you know how to catch a soccer ball pretty easily. And on top of that you have fancy gloves to help you hold onto it. But it's trickier than you think.

Circle the body parts that you think will help you catch the ball.

Elbows	Head	Eyes	Hands
Knees	Legs	Feet	Hips
Fingers	Torso		

Okay, that was an easy one. It's all of them. Use everything you've got to keep the ball from getting into the goal, but keep in mind that all those other body parts are there to help your hands. Don't make the mistake some young players do of using your feet to kick the ball away when you have the opportunity to pick the ball up.

Catching the Ball

Keepers can't afford to make a mistake. In any sport, you might get scored upon if you bobble a catch, but it's not a guarantee. And in baseball or football or basketball you know you're going to turn around and have many other opportunities to score one against the opponents. In soccer, it's different. If the goalie drops the shot, it's probably a goal. And there aren't too many goals that are scored in soccer games.

The keeper catching tips will give you as much security as you can get. The best way to catch a ball depends on how the

Tip

Don't get lazy just because the ball is a slow easy roller. You never know when the ball will hit a bump in the field and pop up. You want your body there to block it.

ball is coming toward you. Let's say it's rolling on the ground. To pick up a rolling ball, follow these basic steps:

1. Move your body behind the ball.
2. Go down on one knee or almost down on one knee.
3. Lean forward.
4. Get your hands down near the ground, palms up, pinkies together.
5. Scoop the ball up and hug it into your chest.
6. Stand up.

Down on the knee
to pick up a ground shot

The reasons behind the first three moves are the same. You're guarding against a miss. If you have your body behind the ball, it acts as a wall. If you get down on one knee, the ball can't go through your legs. If you're leaning forward and the ball bounces out of your hands, then your body knocks it back down and you can dive on it.

If the ball is coming in the air, you want a very different kind of catch. The first step is the same, however. Get your body behind the ball. You need all the help you can to block the ball from going into the goal. Now, however, instead of scooping up the ball, you want your hands out, palms forward rather than facing up. Keep them close together so that your pointer fingers and your thumbs form a W.

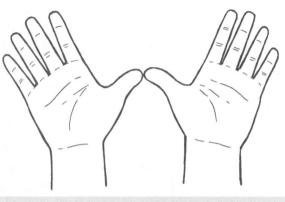

Forming a W with the thumb and forefingers

Keep your elbows bent so when you catch the ball your hands can move back into your chest, taking away some of the impact of the shot. As soon as you've caught the ball, swing your hands around and hug it to your chest.

Those are the easy catches. Unfortunately, there are going to be lots of times when it's going to take all you've got just to get your fingers over to the ball, much less your whole body. Here are some tips to help you deal with those difficult balls:

- ◆ If you have to jump for a ball, go off of one leg. It will get you more height.
- ◆ If you are unsure about being able to grab the ball, tip it over the top or off to the side of the goal.
- ◆ If an opponent is coming in to head the ball at the same time you are trying to catch it, punch the ball away. Your hands can reach higher than her head, but you won't necessarily have the strength or opportunity to pull the ball down into your chest. You can't risk a loose ball in front of the goal, so reach up and punch it out with your fist or fists.
- ◆ If a ball is coming in hard on the ground and you aren't going to be able to go down on one knee to save it, dive. This way your body will act as a barrier.

Getting Rid of the Ball

Okay, you've made your spectacular save. The ball is gripped tightly in between your state-of-the-art gloves. And you have only six seconds to do something with it. What do you do? First, quickly scan the field to make sure there's no one who will benefit from an immediate release. If not, which is most of the time, run out to the 18-yard line. Why waste 16 feet of your punt or throw by standing back in the goal?

Dive, Dive, Dive

It's hard to get used to the idea of throwing yourself on the ground for a diving save. To work up to it, try this with a friend. Kneel on the ground and have your friend throw the ball to one side or the other. Fall on your side as you grab the ball. You'll notice it really doesn't hurt that much. Once you get used to the motion of catching the ball as you fall on your side, you'll have an easier time of diving for it.

Once you're out there you have three options:

1. Kick
2. Throw
3. Roll

The advantage to kicking is that you get it farther away from the goal (and closer to the opponent's goal!), but you can't be as accurate and it can easily end up in the other team's possession. A throw can be much more accurate, but it doesn't go very far. A roll is even more accurate, but it gets you the least amount of distance. So how do you decide?

Since the kick will get the ball farthest down the field, you want to use this when the opponents haven't gotten back quickly and you might gain an advantage down at their end. You also want to use this when the opponents are dominating you. The ball has spent way too much time in your end. Get it out of there.

You can use any kind of kick that works best for you, but most goaltenders find that the punt gets them the most distance. To punt, hold the ball in both hands out in front of your body. Take a hop to plant your nonkicking foot and drop the ball. Your kicking foot should then swing forward and connect with the underside of the ball just before it hits the ground. Follow through with your leg in the direction you want the ball to go.

If the opponents have anticipated your kick and cleared out back to midfield, then you might want to use a roll or a throw. Your teammates should be breaking out toward the touchlines (or sidelines) as soon as you save the ball. Look there for one of them to be open. You should never throw or roll the ball up the middle. It's much too dangerous. Getting the ball over to the side gives you a little more time to recover if the opponents do manage to steal the ball.

Tip

No matter when you're taking a big kick—whether it's a corner kick, a goal kick, or a punt (but especially with a punt)—keep your head down and your eye on the ball the whole time.

Speed Drill

This tiny picture puzzle shows where the goalie is allowed to use her hands. Where is that?

Tip

The bigger the arc you make with your arms when throwing the ball, the farther it will go.

The goalkeeper throw

Use the roll when you have a player fairly near you who has no chance of being intercepted. Give the ball a hard under-handed roll in the direction of your teammate. A roll is nice because it's on the ground and therefore easy to handle. It's also very accurate.

But let's say there is an opponent milling around. It would be dangerous to roll the ball out. In this case, the throw is the better option. It gives you considerably more distance and allows you to get the ball over the head of your opponents.

To make the throw, take one arm back with the ball in that hand. Point the other arm at your target. Take a step with the leg opposite your throwing arm and swing your throwing arm in a wide arc out toward your teammate. As that arm goes up, your outstretched pointing arm should come down. Your hips will twist forward, with your body coming forward after them. Snap your wrist at the last minute as you let go of the ball.

Cutting the Angle

You can cut down on the number of risky saves by paying attention to where you and the shooter are in relation to the goal. If the shooter is coming in from the side, you should move over a little to that side. See what that does to his possible shots on page 61.

If it's a one-on-one breakaway situation, face it: You're in big trouble. But there are a couple of things you can do that are a little more effective than crossing your fingers for luck. The first thing you should do is move slowly toward the dribbling player. Look what happens to the available goal area when you move forward.

But *slowly* is the key word here. You don't want to rush out and have the dribbler fake around you to an open goal. And you don't want him to make an easy chip over your head either. But if you move out slowly, he may feel forced to take a shot at a considerably smaller goal area, or he may make a mistake. However, don't be cautious when he's made a mistake. If you notice that he's dribbled slightly too far out in front of himself and you think you can get the ball, go for it!

Cutting the angle for a player coming in from the side.

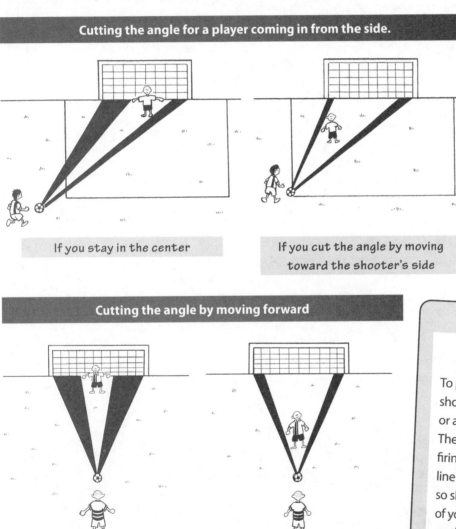

If you stay in the center

If you cut the angle by moving toward the shooter's side

Cutting the angle by moving forward

Staying back

Moving forward

Get in the Net

To practice catching different shots, set up a goal in your yard or against a wall in a playground. Then you and a friend take turns firing balls at each other. Set up a line that the shooter can't cross, so she doesn't get too close. Each of you should take twenty shots on the other. See who makes the most saves. Vary the shots or just practice low balls or high balls.

Communication

The goaltender should be the director on the field. No one can see the entire game as well as you can, and you need to open your big mouth and tell people what you see. If a teammate has time to get the ball under control, yell "Time!" If he needs to get rid of it immediately, yell, "One touch!" or "Man on!" or whatever other term your team uses. Tell your defense to push up if they're hanging back. Call a defender off if you think you can get the ball first. It's much better for the goalkeeper to have the ball under control than for a defender to merely be clearing it out of the goal area.

The keeper needs to communicate during free kicks as well. When the referee calls a direct kick against your team and the ball is down near the goal area, your team will want to set up a wall. This is when your direction is most important, because the kicker doesn't need to wait for the referee's whistle to take her free kick. If you don't set up your wall quickly, then you might not have the opportunity. The defend-

We're with You!

This team is really supporting their keeper! Using a simple number substitution code (A=1, B=2, etc.) figure out what the team is spelling out with the numbers on their jerseys.

ers should know automatically that they need to get into a wall, but they will need your help getting into the right spot, and you need to know how to do it.

First, take the last player on the wall and line her up with the post. Tell her to move left or right until she's covered that whole area of the goal. Every other player should be shoulder to shoulder with that first player. You'll learn more about the field player's role in the wall in the chapter on defensive strategies.

You take the space on the far side of the goal that's left open. Now there's very little space left for the kicker to put her shot. If she tries to chip it over the wall, it won't have much power, which should give you the time you need to move over.

Tip

Because the kicker doesn't need to wait for your wall to set up, your team might want to position the wall too close to the kicker. Now the kicker will wait until the referee moves them back the required 10 feet. This gives your defense chance to get into the right spot.

The wall

Never Blame the Keeper

The one thing you need to learn before you become a goal-keeper, and the one thing that every soccer player should learn before they take the field, is that the goalkeeper cannot be blamed for the loss. The keeper is the last line of defense.

FuN FACT

Tim Howard

One of the best goalkeepers ever to come out of the United States is Tim Howard. He was a super-star in high school and drafted by the NY/NJ Metrostars (now the NY Red Bulls) a year later. His incredible saves attracted international attention, and he became Manchester United's first American player ever. People were skeptical, but Tim Howard was used to proving himself. He's also fought a battle with Tourette's syndrome most of his life.

He's there to save the team from all their mistakes. Think about it. When you start the game, the ball is in the center of the field and there are eleven players on your team between the ball and the goal. It is only after all ten of the field players fail to gain possession of the ball and move it in the other direction that the goalkeeper gets his hands on it. Who's to blame then? Some of the best goalkeeping performances have come from keepers on lousy teams. If a keeper gets 50 shots on goal and saves 48 of them, that's impressive. If his team is only able to get four shots off at the other end and the keeper saves all four, then the score is still a 2–0 loss. But who put in the better goalkeeping performance? I think it was the keeper who saved 48 shots instead of only four.

If you're a field player, listen to your goalkeeper, do whatever you can to keep the ball away from your goalkeeper, and respect your goalkeeper. In fact, in every team game—not just soccer—pointing fingers and laying blame is ruinous. Always support your teammates. Focus on playing the best game you can and remember that even the very best players make mistakes.

JOKIN' AROUND

Question: Why won't Cinderella ever be a great soccer goalkeeper?
Answer: She runs away from the ball.

CHAPTER 6

On the Attack

E ver hear the expression "Possession is nine-tenths of the law"? Well, even if you haven't, remember it now because possession is nine-tenths of soccer strategy. If you have the ball, you want to keep it. If your team can hold on to the ball, then the other team can't shoot. And if they can't shoot, they can't score. Pretty simple.

The hard part comes when you try to figure out how to hold on to that ball once you've got it.

Pass, Pass, Pass

Soccer is a team sport, so be sure to play the game that way. If you constantly pass the ball back and forth between your teammates, the defense is going to have a hard time getting hold of the ball. It's like a giant game of Monkey in the Middle. They'll be running around like chickens with their heads cut off, and you'll be setting yourselves up for a shot on goal. At least that is what we'd like to happen.

Tip

On the kickoff, sometimes the best strategy is to pass back, just to ensure you remain in possession of the ball.

Go for the Cone

A version of Monkey in the Middle called Coneball is a fun way to practice your passing and off-the-ball movement skills. Place a cone in the center of your area. If you have three or four players, have one defender. If you have five, six, or seven players, increase it to two defenders, and so on. For the example, let's do a five-on-two situation. The object of the game is to see if the five players on the outside can hit the cone with the ball. The two defenders try to stop them, but they're not allowed within 3 feet of the cone. The outside players pass the ball around until they get an open shot.

Just because passing is the best offensive strategy, however, that doesn't mean that you should pass every time you get the ball. If the other team is giving you the space to dribble, take it. Force them to commit to guarding you, and you'll be more likely to find someone else open for a pass.

And that brings up another key point of passing. The receiver is just as important as the passer. A receiver might be wide open on the touchlines, but he's completely useless to the passer if there are a couple of defenders between them. Moving when you don't have the ball is just as important as when you have the ball. Run to a spot that's open and in a good line to receive a pass.

One of the key aspects to good passing is having receivers who stay spread out. That way you create some open spaces in the middle to run into. For some reason, the ball is like a magnet to most young players. If you watch a game played by kindergartners, it looks like a swarm of bees has gathered around the ball to move it down the field. It's hard to make a pass if your teammate is 6 inches away. One concept that is helpful is to think of the field like a big sailboat. If everyone runs to one side of the boat it's going to tip over. You need to keep the boat balanced for smooth sailing.

When all is said and done, however, the best offensive weapon you have is your mouth. Talk to your teammates all the time. Let them know if they have time to get the ball under control or if they have to get rid of it quickly. Let them know where you are or where you're going.

Using these terms helps give your teammate a specific idea of where you are. Just yelling, "I'm open" doesn't help as much. And on the flip side, you should only be talking when you actually are open. Don't call for the ball if you have a few defenders between you and your teammate.

Tip

Know what your teammates can do. If the player with the ball can't kick it more than 20 feet, don't stand 40 feet away and call for the ball.

WORDS to KNOW

Here are some typical soccer terms, and here's what they mean:

Back: "I'm behind you."
Cross it: "Send a lofted ball to the center."
Wall: "I'm going to pass the ball to you and then you should pass it right back."
Give-and-go: Same thing as "wall."
Line: "I'm on the touchline or sideline."
Man on: "You don't have time to settle the ball. There's a player on you."
Square: "I'm at a right angle to you."
Switch the field: "Send the ball to the other side of the field."
Time: "You have time to settle the ball."
Through: "Send a ball in between the two defenders and I'll run onto it."

The EVERYTHING KIDS' Soccer Book

Know Your Position

At the start of each game, the coach will give each player a position. Knowing what is expected of each position will help you stay spread out once the game starts. Coaches use a variety of formations, but the positions can be broken down in three basic categories:

- ◆ Forwards
- ◆ Midfielders
- ◆ Defenders

Here are two of the many possible formations:

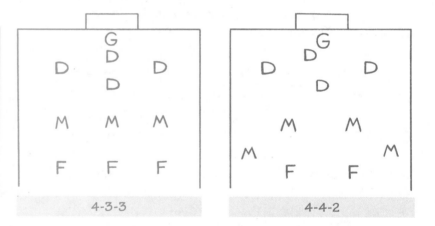

4-3-3   4-4-2

In general, the forwards are always in front of the midfielders who are in front of the defenders, but sometimes players can switch positions. This is why it's good for everyone to have at least some idea of all the positions on the field.

If you're playing midfield and you see a wide-open spot down the sideline, you should sprint into it to receive the ball. Now you might be playing up with the forwards, but someone else can shift into your position until you have a chance to get

Tip

Meet the ball! Let's say you've made a great run into an open space and your teammate passes you the ball. Do you wait for it to come to you? Absolutely not! Go get it.

Name Games

To get people in the habit of talking, play a passing game with names. Mark off a fairly large area and divide the group in half. One half should have balls; the other shouldn't. The group with the balls dribbles around the area until they hear someone call their name. Then they pass to that person and run off and find someone with a ball who they can call to. You can take it up a notch by also having people say "square" or "back" for instance, to describe their location, in addition to the name.

Move the Ball

Dribble your way around the cones from START to GOAL. Avoid bumping into other members from your team who are practicing at the same time.

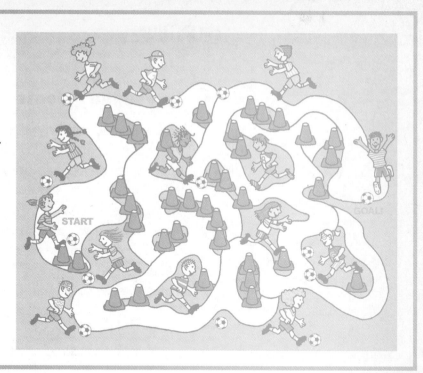

back. Switching positions and making them overlapping is an extremely important part of soccer, but if no one covers for you, you can leave your spot vulnerable. For instance, if a forward is always hanging back with the defenders, then there's no one to receive the ball when it gets into the opponent's half of the field. And if defenders are always running up trying to score, then there is very little protecting the goal. Remember that soccer is a team game, and everyone should be working together to cover all parts of the field.

If you're a player who likes to run all over, then perhaps you should think about playing midfield. While the midfielders generally stay in between the defenders and the forwards, they are expected to go all the way up for the attack and all the way back to defend.

No matter where you play, you should realize that all ten field players are responsible for shooting, passing, and defending. When your team has the ball, everyone is on the attack. When the other team has the ball, everyone is on defense.

WORDS to KNOW

Striker: This player leads the attack. He positions himself on the edge of the defense, ready to sprint forward when his teammates get the ball up to him. Not every team uses a striker, but you should know what it means just in case your coach puts you there.

Spread the Defense

All the positions we've talked about tell you where to be when you're moving up and down the field, but it's also important to be aware of your positioning side to side. If you're on the left side, try not to drift too far into the middle. And if you're over on the right side of the field, you're definitely in the wrong place. In other words, don't tip the boat. Holding your position not only opens up the passing opportunities we discussed earlier, but it helps to spread the defense. If you and your teammates are all spread out, the defense only has two choices.

1. They can spread out with you, playing man to man.
2. They can stay bunched up in the middle protecting their goal.

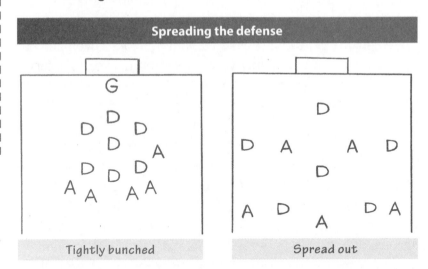

Spreading the defense

Tightly bunched　　　　Spread out

If the defense comes out to the touchlines to make sure they have every player covered, they leave a lot of field space open in the middle. In that case, you and your teammates can make runs through the open middle to receive the ball. If they stay bunched in the middle, then you can dribble the ball unopposed down the side.

However, if your team all crowds the middle, then the defense doesn't have to make that difficult choice. They can bunch in the middle to protect their goal and play man to man at the same time—all because your team has bunched up in the middle.

The tricky part of going wide is that the defenders are going to try to trap you in the corner. You'll need to make a move to the middle well before you get there. Although it's nice to be able to have some space along the touchlines to dribble, you need to get the ball into the middle in order to score. If you see an opportunity at any time once you've passed the centerline, you need to go for it. Your teammate can always bring it back out to the side if he finds it too congested in the middle. A zig-zag pattern down the field is quite effective.

One of the best ways to get the ball into the center is a *cross*. If you find yourself a step ahead of the defender, turn in toward the goal and send a high lofted pass to one of your teammates who should be waiting for the cross in front of the goal. The ideal cross should come down in front of the goal right in the vicinity of your teammate's head. Then he can put his forehead on it and redirect it into the goal. A cross can also be on the ground if you have open field to make the pass.

Spreading the defense will work even right in front of the goal. If your teammate is bringing the ball up the middle, don't stand in the middle waiting for him to pass to you. Start running out to the edge of the box. If a defender doesn't follow you, then you're wide open for a pass

Tip

When you're down in front of the goal, you have to make sure that your runs wide don't put you offside.

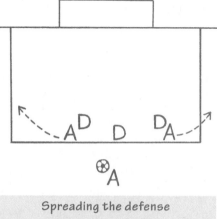

Spreading the defense
in front of the goal

71

and then a shot. If he does, then you've cleared out the middle for your teammate with the ball. Either way, there's a good chance you'll get a shot off.

Escaping the Guard

If a defender is doing her job right, she will make it very difficult for you to even receive the ball, especially when you're right in front of the goal. So you're going to have to figure out a way to lose her. If you stand still, she can guard you easily. If you run around, she has to follow. Movement is your best weapon. You know where you're going next. She doesn't. Just make sure your moves are quick and sharp. A long, loopy jog around won't give the defender any difficulty.

Look at this figure and you can see one example of how to do this. To start, run straight at the person who is bringing the ball down the field. If your defender follows you, she's leaving space in the goal area. At some point in your run, stop and run off to the side and back toward the goal. If your teammate is playing heads-up ball, she'll pass right at that moment and you'll have the ball free and clear. Take that shot!

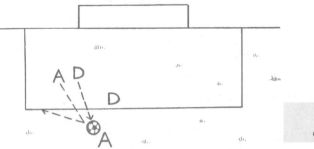

Losing a
defender

Keep in mind that the success of this play depends as much on the timing of the passer as it does on the running of the receiver. If you're the one with the ball, you have to always be paying attention to what your teammates are doing.

The More the Merrier

To spice up the game of soccer a little and give you and your teammates more opportunity to score, throw a few more soccer balls into a regular game of soccer. Now people really have to be looking up and paying attention to all parts of the field. If you can handle two balls, then add a third. See how many balls you can add to your game without it getting out of control.

Speed Drill

You're wide open for a pass—what do you do? This tiny picture puzzle shows you!

Hi! How do you do?

Offensive Dos and Don'ts for Restarts

When the ball goes out of bounds or a player commits a foul, the other team gets a free kick or throw-in. Even though there's only one player taking the kick or the throw, the whole team has a job to do.

CORNER KICK

DO

- ⚽ Loft the ball into the center of the goal area
- ⚽ Use your head to take the shot
- ⚽ Move around to get open

DON'T

- ⚽ Use a kicker who isn't strong enough
- ⚽ Wait for the ball to land
- ⚽ Stand in one spot waiting for the ball

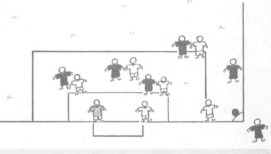

The corner kick

DIRECT KICK

DO

- ⚽ Take the shot as quickly as possible; there's no whistle, so don't wait for one
- ⚽ Go for the shot if you're near the goal

DON'T

- ⚽ Wait for the defense to set up a wall or mark up
- ⚽ Waste a shot opportunity by passing it off

WORDS to KNOW

Restart: Occurs after play has been stopped because of the referee's whistle. Restarts include corner kicks, goal kicks, direct kicks, indirect kicks, kickoffs, and throw-ins.

INDIRECT KICK

DO

- Have one player tap the ball and a second follow behind and shoot it
- If they set up a wall, take advantage of the unmarked players on your team and make a pass.

DON'T

- Have your first player shoot it; the keeper can let it in if only one person has touched it, and it won't count as a goal.
- Get intimidated because they have a wall. In this case it's to your advantage.

THROW-INS

DO

- Throw it as soon as you can; there's no whistle to wait for unless there is a substitution.
- Throw it at your teammate's feet if she's close to you. Loft it high and as far as you can if the defense is in front.
- Throw it down the line if you're near the goal you're defending.
- Throw it in the middle if you're near the opponent's goal.

DON'T

- Wait for the defense to set up.
- Throw it so hard that your teammate can't handle it easily, especially when she's close to you.
- Throw it down the line if you're in front of the opponent's goal.
- Throw it in the middle if you're in front of your own goal.

Opposite Offense

Here's a funny conversation between two soccer players. All the words that are underlined actually mean the opposite! Above each underlined word or group of words, write a word that means the opposite.

"Hey <u>here</u>, Lucas!"

"<u>Good-bye</u>, Caitlin!"

"How are <u>me</u>?"

"<u>You</u> <u>haven't</u> a <u>good</u> <u>hot</u>."

"How <u>wonderful</u>! I hope you <u>give</u> <u>worse</u> <u>a long time from now</u>."

"<u>You</u>, too. I <u>did</u> <u>wake</u> <u>none</u> <u>day</u> <u>short</u>."

"Oh, that's too <u>good</u>.

Well, <u>you</u> <u>haven't</u> to <u>come</u>. <u>Hello</u>!"

"<u>Hello</u>. See <u>me</u> <u>sooner</u>."

Super Soccer

The game of soccer didn't have one set of rules until the 1800s. Before that time it was a popular game in many English schools, but each school had slightly different rules. However, all the schools agreed on one thing—the ball could never be touched by the player's hands. That's why in England, and in many other countries, the game we call soccer is still called "football"!

Help the player with the ball run around the defense to score.

That's
A-Maze-Ing!

Games in which balls are kicked have been popular for centuries. Early balls were made from all sorts of things—solid balls of rubber or wood, balls of straw wrapped with wool and feathers, even pig bladders!

CHAPTER 7
Defense

FUN FACT

Beijing Olympics

Sometimes defense can matter more than offense. In the gold medal game in the 2008 Olympics, the United States played an outstanding Brazilian team. Brazil dominated the game, but the U.S. defenders were up to the job. The score was 0–0 at the end of regulation play. Then, in the sixth minute of overtime, U.S. player Carli Lloyd got a pass from Amy Rodriguez and took a shot at the far post for a goal. The U.S. defenders hung in there for the rest of overtime, and the U.S. won 1–0.

Speed Drill

This tiny number puzzle shows a popular kind of defense. What is it?

1
one

Defending the goal is more than just the goalkeeper's job. It's the job of every single player on the field. In fact, if the ball even gets to the keeper, it means that ten other people failed at what they were supposed to be doing.

You have two purposes when you're defending: you want to stop the other team's attack, and you want to take the ball away from them. Working as a team can help you to achieve both of those goals. But first you need to learn how to be a good defender.

Defensive Skills

Good defense starts with good individual skills. Defenders need balance, focus, and patience, and they need to use their heads. Speed, strength, and skills help, too, of course, but that goes for *everyone* on the field.

Balance is primary. It's tough to stay on a player when he's trying every move in the book: changing speeds, changing directions, and faking you out. You have to react. You have no idea where he's going next. The best way to do this is to stay low, with your legs apart and your knees bent. Your arms should be out rather than at your sides. All of this will help you keep your balance as you're forced to change directions quickly.

Part of defense is focus. You need to have all your attention on the ball. You can't let your mind wander because you might have to react in a split second. Watch the ball and only the ball. Don't

The defensive stance

become distracted by the fakes the attacker is trying to make with her body. It doesn't matter if her body is leaning to the left or lunging to the right. If her feet aren't moving, then neither is the ball. Watch the ball, and react only when the ball moves.

In fact, much of defense is a waiting game. You don't want to make a move until you're sure you can get the ball. If you overcommit too early, the dribbler will be around you in a heartbeat. You want to wait for her to make a mistake. The second she lets the ball get a little too far away, pounce on it.

And finally a smart heads-up defender can steal a lot of balls by paying attention to what her attackers are doing. If you notice that someone never passes with her left foot, then cut off her right side and force her to use her left. If you have a lot of speed, you can step away from the player you're guarding, leaving her slightly "open" for a pass and then zip in and intercept the pass when it comes. Force the players wide if they don't have a good cross. If the other team is very good, then stay back so they don't get a breakaway. A smart, focused defender is invaluable to her team.

Containing and Controlling

Sometimes you're not right on top of the ball; instead, you have an attacker coming at you and heading for the goal with the ball under his control. In this case, your behavior is slightly different. The first thing you want to do is slow him down. This is especially important if he's on a breakaway and you have to wait for the rest of your teammates to catch up and get back to defend. By slowing the attacker down, you're giving your teammates a chance to get back and help. This is called *containment*.

One-on-One Basics

If you and a friend want to practice soccer, a little one-on-one game will help you work on lots of skills, especially defense. A piece of advice, though: Don't make your goals more than 20 feet apart, or you're going to be exhausted. If you have four people, you might want to have two people be the goals (if they spread their legs wide, you can kick it through their legs) and two people play one on one. After a goal, you switch up. That way you get some rest because one-on-one is very tiring.

WORDS to KNOW

Containment: The process of slowing down an attacker and keeping him in front of you as you back toward the goal.

Speed Drill

This tiny picture puzzle shows a defense against a direct kick. What is it?

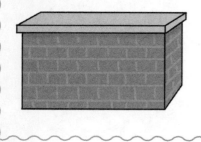

As the player approaches you, you move in and approach him, too. You want to move quickly, but you don't want an all-out sprint here because then you'll have a harder time adjusting to what the dribbler does. Your momentum will still be taking you forward. You want to move in as fast as you can while still being able to stop on a dime.

When you get within 4 or 5 feet of the player, go into your defensive stance. Just like before, stay low, with your knees bent and your legs apart. Keep your arms out wide for balance and lean forward. Now back up slowly. The attacker will have to slow down because you're in front of him.

You have to focus on keeping your body between him and the goal. Containment gives your teammates time to get into their defensive positions, and it also can force the attacker to make a mistake. He might pass the ball too soon or make a dribbling error. Whatever you do, don't move in to steal the ball until you know your teammates are in a position to help out and you're sure you can get it. The last thing you want is to have him fake around you and have a breakaway toward the goal.

If the rest of the defense is in place, then you don't have to worry so much about containment. Now you need to try to

Forcing an attacker to the side

challenge and control the player. Still in your defensive stance, try to angle your body to push the player toward the side. The closer he is to the touchline, the worse his angle is for the goal. Plus, you may be able to trap him against the line or in the corner and force him to kick the ball out-of-bounds. If you block off the access to the goal, but leave space open on the side, that's where he'll naturally end up going.

Defensive Formations

As mentioned in the last chapter, everyone plays offense when your team has the ball, and everyone plays defense when you don't. But some positions are generally considered more defensive than others, which is why they are called defenders. Like basketball, defense in soccer can be either man-to-man or zone.

Man-to-Man

If you're playing man-to-man defense, you'll want to pick a player from the other team and stay with her. This is called *marking up*. If your player has the ball, then you want to mark her tightly. If you need to allow your teammates a chance to get into position, then you contain your player, but if you feel you have lots of backup, you move in tighter and challenge her. Force her to look down at the ball, so she can't see her teammates. Make sure you keep your body between the opponent and the goal.

If your player doesn't have the ball, then you need to stay with her but not as tightly. You want to deny her the ball, but you also need to be in a position to help out your teammates if someone breaks free. The farther away you are from the ball, the farther you can be from the player you're marking.

WORDS to KNOW

Marking up: Another term for man-to-man defense. That means you cover a player rather than an area, staying with them no matter where they go.

WORDS to KNOW

Zone defense: Covering an area rather than a person. You pick up the player who goes into that area.

Attack!

To practice working with another defender, you might want to try this exercise for four players. Have two players stand on a line (the defenders) and two across from them about 30 feet away (the attackers). The defenders start with the ball and pass it to the attackers. The attackers then try to get the ball back over the line. Meanwhile, the defenders move forward, working together. One of them should call "Ball" and move in close to force the player with the ball to make a move. The other defender stays back with an eye on the open attacker, but he is also looking to pick up the one with the ball if he happens to dribble around the first defender. If the defenders get the ball away, they get a point. If the attackers get it over the line, they get a point. Play up to 10 and then switch roles.

Zone Defense

Sometimes coaches prefer to have a zone defense. In this case the players are covering an area, not a person. The defender on the left side covers the left side, the defender in the middle takes the middle, the defender on the right side takes the right side, etc.

Most coaches these days have a zone formation with four defenders. The player nearest the ball moves in to directly confront the attacker. The next closest player becomes the backup in case the defender gets beaten. He should move in toward the action but not get so close that he interferes. The third and fourth players are farther off the ball, so they can see the whole field and where the opponents might be bringing in their attack, but they are shifting as well. It's as if the defense is setting up wall after wall after wall for the attackers to go through.

If you're playing zone, then you need to make sure you communicate well. One person needs to move forward and confront the player with the ball. Usually it's the person defending that zone. He should yell "Ball!" and make his move. Then the rest of the defenders know that they are responsible for covering his area, and they shift accordingly. If the ball is passed into another zone, then somebody else picks up the dribbler and the first defender slips back into zone mode. It takes a lot of teamwork, but it can be a very effective defense.

Guidelines for Both

There are two defensive positions—sweeper and stopper—that have specific jobs all on their

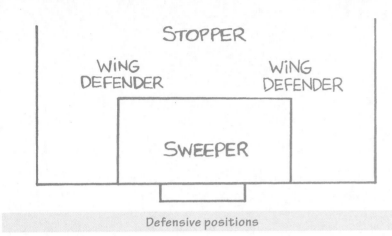

STOPPER

WING
DEFENDER

WING
DEFENDER

SWEEPER

Defensive positions

own. Not every team uses these two positions, but many do, whether they play man-to-man or zone.

The *stopper* is the first line of defense. If you're a stopper it means that your coach thinks you're very aggressive and can be tough on the opponents. If you're playing man-to-man defense, this person usually marks up with the striker from the other team. If you're playing zone, the stopper will usually be the first one to confront any ball coming toward your half of the field.

The *sweeper* is the last line of defense. She should be very fast and willing to move all over. She's the cleanup player, getting balls if they should get through the rest of the defense. Having a sweeper to back up the defense allows the defenders to be a little more aggressive on offense.

Remember, all 11 players are part of both the attack and the defense. Even if the ball is far away from your goal, you'll still have a job to do as a defender. Remember the offsides rule? The other team can't keep an attacker in your half of the field if there are no defenders there. So move on up! Push the opponents back to their goal. If your team is attacking their goal, then all your defenders should at least be at the midfield line.

WORDS to KNOW

Stopper: This player is the first line of defense, but can also be a significant force on offense. It works best if this player is a loud-mouth, take-charge person.

Sweeper: This is the cleanup player (which is why the name is so appropriate). She's the last line of defense before the keeper.

Defensive Lineup

This defensive lineup has five players, arranged from shortest to tallest. Read the clues to figure out who plays which position.

The goalie is taller than the wing.
The fullback is taller than the sweeper.
The sweeper is taller than the stopper.
The wing is taller than the fullback.

Patty   Ben   Jamal   Flo   Josh

Defense Against Restarts

After having read the previous chapter on what the offense should be doing, you might be able to figure out what the defense should be doing for the restarts, but here's an easy table to give you all the answers:

KICK	DEFENSIVE RESPONSE
Corner kick	One player should take the near post, the goalkeeper should be on the far post, and a defender should be looking for the short ball. Everyone else marks up.
Direct kick	Set up a wall in front of the kick.
Indirect kick	Mark up tightly and be prepared for the second kicker to shoot.
Goal kick	Go wide to the touchline. Do not kick the ball in front of the goal.
Throw-in	Mark up and look for the ball to come down the line.

If you'll notice, most of the restarts have you marking up man-to-man. You should do this even if you're playing a zone defense. Your goal is to try to beat the other team to the ball and clear it away from your goal area.

Tip

When you're defending against a corner kick, you should try to stand slightly in front of the person you're guarding. That way you can get to the ball first. Be careful, however, that she doesn't slip away because she's behind you. Be looking at her out of the corner of your eye.

The Wall

Making a wall in front of a direct kick is a valuable defensive tool, but you don't want to use it until you have it mastered. A weak wall is worse than no wall at all, because you've taken four or five of your defensive players and put them all in one spot. Here are the key points.

1. Listen to your goalkeeper. He will tell you how many players he wants in the wall and he will line you up.
2. Stand as close to the kick as you're allowed, which is 10 yards. Move in closer than that to start and let the referee move you back. This will give your whole defense time to get in position.
3. The end player should be blocking the goalpost on one side. The keeper will tell you to move right or left if you're not right there.
4. Everyone else should line up shoulder-to-shoulder, and so tight that the ball cannot get through.
5. The minute the ball is kicked, break up and defend as normal.

A goalie catching a kicked ball

Go Team!

These fans want everyone to know how much they love the game!
Follow the directions below to find out their mighty message.

1. Fill in all the blocks on the left side of signs 1, 2, 3, 6, 7, 9, 11, 12, 15, 21
2. Fill in all the top squares on signs 2, 3, 5, 6, 9, 11, 15, 16, 21
3. Fill in all the bottom squares of signs 1, 2, 3, 9, 11, 12, 16
4. Fill in all the right squares of signs 1, 6, 11, 12
5. Fill in all the squares down the middle of signs 5 and 8

6. Fill in the very middle square of signs 1, 6, 7, 16, 21
7. Fill in the square just below the middle square of sign 1
8. Copy sign 9 onto sign 18 and 19
9. Copy sign 5 onto sign 13
10. Copy sign 7 onto sign 10
11. Copy sign 2 onto sign 4 and 20
12. Copy sign 11 onto sign 17 and 14

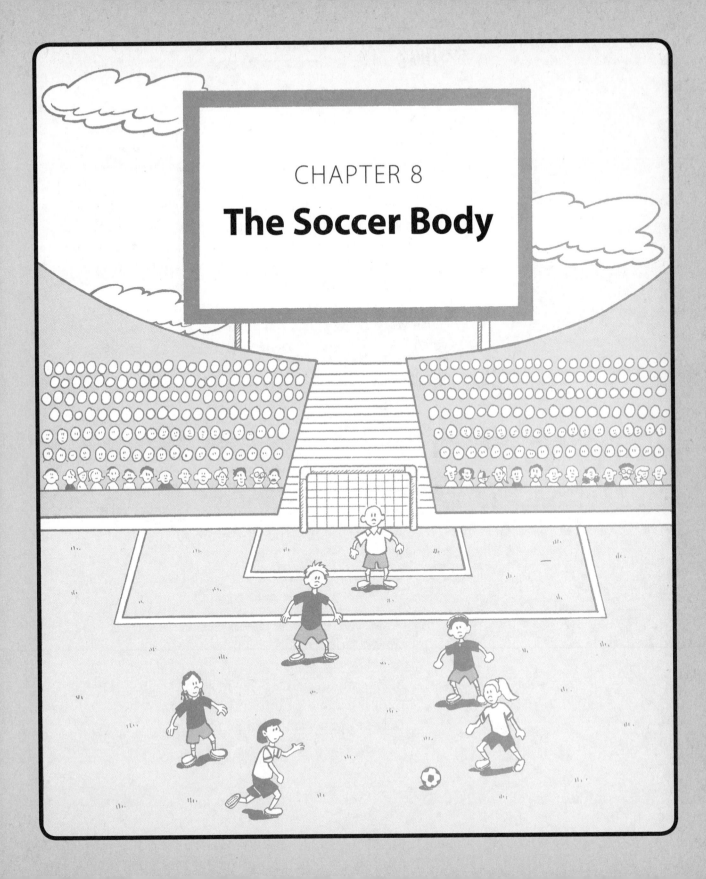

CHAPTER 8

The Soccer Body

Soccer can be rough on your body. Sprained ankles, pulled muscles, and lots of bumps and bruises are just part of the game. But soccer can also be great for your body. It builds endurance, improves your coordination, and gives your heart and lungs some good exercise. Whether it makes you hurt or healthy is largely up to you. Knowing your body's needs and limitations is an important part of playing sports. Read this chapter to find out how to deal with some common soccer fitness and injury problems.

First, let's have some fun. Take this little quiz and see how much you already know. You might know more than you think you do. A lot of these answers will take you by surprise!

1. How far does a soccer player run in an average soccer game?
   A. 100 yards
   B. 1 mile
   C. 5 miles
   D. As much as a marathon

2. What's the best way to prevent a muscle pull?
   A. Stretch before and after exercising
   B. Lift weights
   C. Sit in front of the TV
   D. Ice your muscles before you play

3. When you're outside playing soccer, when is the best time to drink water?
   A. Before you get thirsty
   B. The minute you feel you're getting thirsty
   C. At least an hour after you get thirsty
   D. Never, you should drink milk

4. What is the best drink when you're hot and thirsty?
   A. Milk
   B. Juice
   C. Soda
   D. Water or a sports drink

5. What is the MOST serious thing that can happen to your body on a hot day?
   A. Sunburn
   B. Heat exhaustion
   C. Heat stroke
   D. Sweat

6. What should you do if you sprain your ankle?
   A. Put ice on it
   B. Elevate it
   C. Wrap it tightly
   D. All of the above

7. What's the worst thing you could do if someone knocks out one of your teeth?
   A. Wash it with warm soapy water
   B. Put it in a glass of milk
   C. Put it in your mouth
   D. Smile

8. Which one of these is NOT a sign of a concussion?
   A. Different-size pupils
   B. Bleeding
   C. Dizziness
   D. Vomiting

The answers are 1–C, 2–A, 3–A, 4–D, 5–C, 6–D, 7–A, 8–B. If you got any of them wrong or even if you didn't, read on for more details about all of those issues and more soccer-related fitness and injury advice.

Warm Up

These two players know that it's important to warm up before a game. Player "L" is going to run slowly around the field, touching all the light colored dots. Player "D" is going to touch all the dark dots on the field. Follow their paths from number to number with your pencil and you will see a winning soccer move!

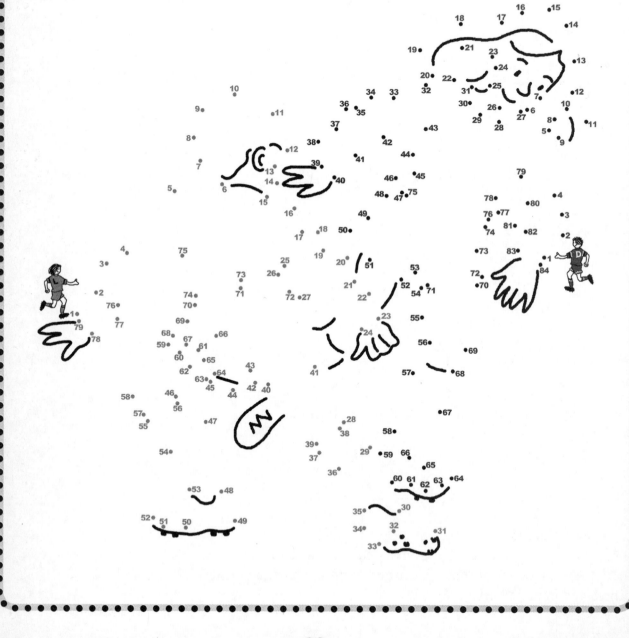

Getting in Shape

Endurance, strength, and flexibility are the three parts of getting in shape, and soccer requires all three. Playing the game itself will build your muscles, and until you're a teenager that's about all the strength training you should do. But even at a very young age, you can work on your endurance and your flexibility.

Endurance

An official soccer game is 90 minutes long. That's 90 minutes of running! One study showed that the average adult soccer player ran about 5 miles in a game.

If you're the kind of kid who's always playing a ton of sports and running around everywhere, then running 5 miles might not seem like too big a deal. But if you're a kid who takes life a little slower, then soccer is something you'll need to build up to. Walk to school instead of getting a ride, or play soccer in the park or backyard instead of playing on the computer. You can really get fit by going running, but even just playing the game will help you build your aerobic capacity.

If you are out of breath in a game, you can find moments when the ball is away from you to take a breather. But don't make the mistake of walking on the field when you should be running. When you're out there, you should be giving it everything you've got. It's better to play hard and then come out and rest than to only give half an effort. You won't have as much fun and you won't help your team much. Tell your coach you need to be subbed. Take a break. Then the next time you go in the game, see if you can push yourself a little more. Eventually, you'll be in the shape you need to be in to be a good player.

Stretching

The other great thing you can do for your body is stretch out those muscles. Most kids don't have tight muscles, and in fact most youth leagues can go an entire season without an injury, but it's never too early to get in the habit of stretching. It keeps your muscles loose and flexible so they won't be caught tight and surprised when you suddenly twist them in a weird direction. Almost every adult soccer player is familiar with the sharp pain of a torn muscle.

Here are some great stretches:

- **Calf stretch:** Lean against a wall or fence, with your feet about a foot and a half away. Press your heels to the ground, one at a time.
- **Front-of-thigh stretch:** Bend your knee and grab your foot from behind. Pull up until you feel the stretch. Switch legs.
- **Inner-thigh stretch:** Sit on the ground. Put the soles of your feet together and press your knees to the ground.
- **Back-of-thigh stretch:** Cross one leg over the other. Bend over and touch the ground. Switch legs.

Water Works!

Your body is flooded with water. But when you exercise, you lose a lot of that water. You have to make sure that you put it back or your body won't function as well.

So how do you know how much water to drink and when to drink it? The answer will probably surprise you. You should drink water all the time. You can have eight to ten glasses of water a day and it wouldn't be too much. And don't wait until you're thirsty. When you feel thirsty it means your body is already short of water. So before a soccer match, drink some

water. On every break, drink some water. After the game, drink some water. Your body will thank you, and you'll have a lot more energy for the game.

A lot of players like to drink sports drinks, and as long as you don't drink too many of them, they'll be just as good as water. Many of them also have electrolytes, which your body loses when it sweats. So they put that back in your body, which is nice. They're also full of water. Soda is not a good idea because it's full of sugar, has very little replenishing value, and the carbonation might make you uncomfortable when you run.

Heat Kills

Water is good for other reasons, too. It will keep your body cool on hot days. Very hot days are uncomfortable, but they can also be dangerous. If you're playing on a hot day, you need to make sure your body temperature doesn't get too high. When your body gets overheated, you can get heat exhaustion or heat stroke. Take breaks, sit in the shade, and pour water on your head.

Heat exhaustion is the less serious one. It basically means you haven't been doing your job drinking enough water and your body is dehydrated. You'll know you have heat exhaustion if you get one of these symptoms:

◆ Excessive thirst
◆ Headache
◆ Dizziness

The cure for heat exhaustion is to stop what you're doing, sit in the shade or get into air conditioning, and slowly drink lots of liquids. Don't gulp. The sudden cold liquid might be too much for your overheated body.

FUN FACT

Water Means Energy!

Most people don't know it, but if you don't have enough water in your body, you tend to be tired and cranky. So next time you're in a bad mood, try drinking a couple of bottles of water. There's a very good chance you'll be happier and have a lot more energy to boot.

Liquid Measure

For one day, keep track of exactly how much you drink. If you have a soda, that's 12 ounces. If you have a big water bottle, that's probably around 20 ounces. A glass of orange juice at breakfast might be about 8 ounces. Add them up and see how well you're doing at keeping your body supplied with liquids.

FUN FACT

Stinky Fact

Have you noticed how grownups get all stinky and sweaty after they work out a lot? And have you noticed that kids don't? That's because until they are teenagers, kids don't have fully developed sweat glands. It's good news because you don't smell, but mostly it means that you have to make sure to keep yourself cool in other ways.

Heat stroke is much more serious. It's a killer. Every year people die from heat stroke: some are hiking in the Grand Canyon without carrying enough water; some are overdressed, overworked, and overweight at midsummer football practices; and some are running marathons and pushing themselves too far to get to the finish line. I have one thing to say to these people and to anyone reading this book: Pay attention to your body's clues!

Your body will tell you if it's not working right. Before you even get to heat stroke, you'll probably experience heat exhaustion and the symptoms you read about there. But if you ignore those and keep pushing yourself, here's what will happen:

◆ You will run a fever.
◆ You will stop sweating.
◆ You will become disoriented.

That last clue is probably the biggest one, but unfortunately if you're the one who is disoriented, you're not going to be able to help yourself too well. So look out for your friends and they'll look out for you. If you see someone with these symptoms, splash her with water, put ice on her neck, and rush her to the hospital. You have to cool her body down before it starts shutting down.

Enough with the really serious, depressing stuff. Most people will drink plenty of fluids and pay attention to what their body is telling them. It's just important for soccer players to know this, since they do a lot of running out in the hot sun.

Ouch!

Heat isn't the only thing that can put a soccer player on the sideline. Injuries are way more often the cause. Muscles get

WORDS to KNOW

Ligaments: The connectors between your bones. Ligaments also support organs and connect cartilage to bones.

94

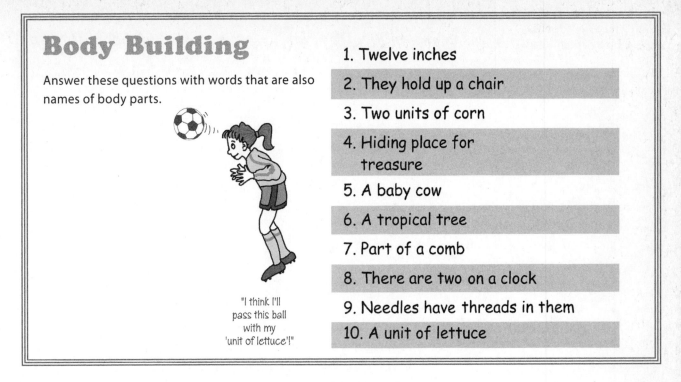

Body Building

Answer these questions with words that are also names of body parts.

"I think I'll pass this ball with my 'unit of lettuce'!"

1. Twelve inches
2. They hold up a chair
3. Two units of corn
4. Hiding place for treasure
5. A baby cow
6. A tropical tree
7. Part of a comb
8. There are two on a clock
9. Needles have threads in them
10. A unit of lettuce

pulled; ligaments get stretched or torn; and bumps and bruises pop up everywhere.

If you're injured, sit down. The referee will see you pretty quickly. If someone else is injured, keep playing until the referee blows his whistle. He has to wait until the ball goes out-of-bounds or until the injured person's team has the ball. This is because otherwise someone might cheat (though we certainly hope not!) and fake an injury just as the ball is nearing the goal. Once the whistle is blown, then you can sit down, too, and wait for the coaches and trainers to deal with the injured player. You can even come to the touchline and get a drink if there's enough time. Just don't leave the field, because the clock is still ticking.

Pulls

Muscles are made up of lots of fibers. They get stretched and pulled every which way when you play soccer. Most of the time they seem to deal with all this activity pretty well, but

Tip

Once you've sprained something, it's going to be weak. Let it heal completely and strengthen the muscles around it or you could have trouble with it for the rest of your life.

WORDS to KNOW

Sprain: A stretching or tearing of a ligament.

Concussion: An injury to the head, particularly the brain, frequently involving a loss of consciousness and dizziness. Symptoms can last up to two weeks after the hit and include difficulty following a conversation, headache, sleeping, and more. The after-effects are called post-concussion syndrome.

sometimes the muscle refuses to move, and that's when you get a pulled muscle. A pulled muscle is just a tear in the muscle fiber. As awful as that sounds, most muscle tears aren't that bad. In fact, you make little tears in your muscles all the time and don't even notice them. That's how muscles grow. So slight muscle pulls shouldn't slow you down one bit. But if you do have a big pull, give your muscle a rest until it no longer hurts.

Sprains

Ligaments will give you a little more of a problem. When you stretch your ligaments, it's called a sprain. Sprains happen when a joint, like your ankle or your knee, is forced to bend too far or in the wrong way. It's a pretty common soccer injury.

The cure for sprains is a process called RICE. It stands for **R**est, **I**ce, **C**ompression, and **E**levation. That basically means get off your feet, put ice on the injury, wrap it tightly, and put the injured part up so too much blood doesn't flow to the area.

Sometimes a ligament is torn; that's much more serious than a sprain. It might heal itself or you might need surgery. At the very least, your soccer playing is over for the season. The more you strengthen and stretch, the less likely you'll have a serious injury.

Heads Up!

Because headers are part of the game, at least once a season someone is going to bang you in the head. Most of the time you'll just say ouch and keep going, but sometimes it's a little more serious than that.

Every time you're hit in the head hard, you have to worry about having a concussion. A concussion is basically a brain bruise. Most of the hits to your head will just end up bruising on the surface. The skull does a really good job protecting your brain. But sometimes the hit is so hard, your brain gets a tiny bit injured. That's a concussion, and you have to look out for it.

Some signs of a concussion include:

◆ Vomiting
◆ Dizziness or walking unsteadily
◆ Different-size pupils or pupils that don't react to light
◆ Talking that makes no sense
◆ Losing consciousness

If you have a few of these symptoms, get checked by a doctor. The doctor can make sure that you haven't cracked your skull or have bleeding in your brain. If you don't have these symptoms but are still worried because the hit was so hard, have someone keep an eye on you for about a day, looking for what might develop. Even at night, they should wake you up every couple of hours.

Injuries are part of sports, but don't worry. If you're careful, they don't have to be serious. Remember to stretch your muscles, pay attention to what your body is telling you, use RICE when you get an injury, and don't push yourself to play when you've been hurt. There's a great rule of thumb to help you know when to say when. It's called the Five-Minute Rule. If you get hurt or you feel dizzy or anything like that, take a break for five minutes. If you're still not feeling right, then you have a more serious injury and should stop playing. If you feel pretty good, get back in the game!

FUN FACT

Save a Tooth

Every once in a while, players think they're going head to head for a soccer ball and they end up going head to tooth! Ouch! What do you do when a tooth gets knocked out? Believe it or not, a glass of milk is the solution. Put the tooth in milk and rush to the hospital or dentist. If you can't find milk, then pop the tooth in your mouth to keep it wet with your saliva. Just don't swallow it! Whatever you do, however, don't wash the tooth in water. That's a sure way to kill it.

Tip

If you have had a really hard blow to the head, stop playing for the day, even if you don't think you have a concussion. A second hit to the same spot could really do some damage.

Spelling Ball

How many words can you find in this soccer ball grid? Start at any letter, then move from one space to the next touching space in any direction, spelling out a word as you go. You may double back and use a letter more than once in a word. For example, you may spell the word EVE.

However, you may not use the same letter twice in a row. For example, you are not allowed to spell SLEEP:

The ten-letter bonus word completes this phrase: Playing soccer is much more fun than watching _____!

SCORE:

10 words = Starter

20 words = Pro

30 words = World Cup

Secret Soccer

Be on the lookout for the word SOCCER hiding in this grid! There is only one time where all six letters appear correctly. Look forward, backward, up, down, and diagonally.

```
S R O S O S O C C E
O O R O S O C C E S
C E C C O C C O R O
C S O C E C E S O C
R O S E R E R O S S
S S O C C O S E O O
O C C S O C E C C C
C E R O C O C C C E
C O O C S E O O S E
E C O S R O C C O S
```

CHAPTER 9

Playing the Game

Playing for Real

Soccer games are fun, but they teach you real skills. See if you can find fifteen skills hidden in the following letter grid. When you have circled all the skills, read the left-over letters from left to right, top to bottom to find one more!

catch	kick	shoot
defend	pass	stretch
dribble	plan	think
fake	receive	trap
juggle	run	volley

```
C P V O L L E Y T S
R A L O C C E R K D
R E T A I S A I D E
E K C C N P C R A F
L N L E H K I L A E
G I B O I B U T C N
G H O P B V E N N D
U T A L T R E K U O
J S E S H O O T A R
S L H C T E R T S F
```

The thrill of victory and the agony of defeat. The sweet feeling of success when you score that goal in the last second of play. The dive in the dirt to tip the ball around the goalpost for a save. Let's face it. The drama of competition is half the fun of playing any sport. Of course, people have different thoughts about competition. Here are a few quotes that you can think about:

> "It doesn't matter if you win or lose, it's how you play the game."
>   or
> "It doesn't matter if you win or lose, as long as you win."

Those are two opposite philosophies, but I think everyone would agree with a third quote:

> "It doesn't matter if you win or lose, it's THAT you played the game."

Adding competition makes most sports more fun. Practicing dribbling or shooting can be fun for a short while, but then it gets dull. You need to have a little challenge.

Pick-Up Games

You don't have to belong to a team to play soccer. Just get out there and play. In fact, most of the world's children play "pick-up" soccer, rather than organized soccer. Pick-up soccer has a bunch of advantages, but here are three good ones:

1. You can play whenever you want.
2. You play with different age kids, so it teaches you to fight hard for the ball, especially if you're one of the younger ones.
3. It's usually a smaller group than the normal 11-on-11 game, so you get to touch the ball more.

Find a backyard, park, or field, and grab a ball. All it takes is at least four people and a little organization. Divide into two teams. Use cones, sweatshirts, sticks, or anything else you can find to make two goals. Then start playing some soccer.

For variety, you can try other games with your group of friends. These will all help you with soccer skills, and the variation might keep it more interesting.

Cats and Dogs

This is a great game for dribbling and defensive skills, and it can be played with any number of players. You'll need to mark off a playing area, but there are no goals. Divide into two teams: the cats and the dogs. Every player on the cat team should have a ball. The dogs do not have balls.

Someone should have a stopwatch or a watch and say, "Go." At that point, the cats dribble around the playing area, shielding, faking, and turning. In other words, they're doing anything they can to keep the dogs away. The dogs are trying to kick all the balls out of the playing area. When they succeed, stop the watch. Now it's the cats' turn to see if they can beat the time while the dogs do the dribbling.

This is a quick game, so you can trade back and forth four or five times and see who gets the fastest time in the end.

Tip

Instead of calling the teams "Cats" and "Dogs," call them by your favorite MLS or WUSA teams. You can say it's a game of Breakers and CyberRays. Or if you follow World Cup soccer more than U.S. soccer, it can be France against Brazil.

Square soccer

Square Soccer

Here's a game you can play with 4–8 people. Set up four cones in a square and divide your friends into two teams. The more people you have, the bigger your square should be. One team takes two touching sides of the square, and the other team takes the other two sides.

The object of the game is not to let the ball go over the line you're defending. You are not allowed into the square, but you may move up and down your line. If everyone is defending too well, then make it a little more difficult by adding more balls.

Two-Goal Soccer

This game could be looked at as a variation on square soccer. In this game, you want to use your cones (or sweatshirts or whatever you use to make goals) to make four goals, rather than the four sides of a square. The four goals, however, do form a square. Now, instead of defending the two sides of your square, you're defending your two goals, and you are now allowed "inside" the square.

Youth League Soccer

Because soccer is such a simple game, kids can start playing as soon as they're able to kick a ball. This makes it the perfect sport for youth leagues, and many towns and cities provide a variety of organized soccer leagues for children. In addition, high schools and middle schools frequently have teams. If this is something that interests you, do some research. Find out if your town has youth league soccer programs. They may even have more than one type.

Recreation Leagues

Some towns have "rec" leagues, or in-town leagues. This is a great way to begin playing soccer. The teams are usually made up of kids all in the same town and they're divided as equally as possible; the uniforms are probably different colored T-shirts. The teams might have one practice and one game a week and are usually coached by parents. More often than not, the goal is to learn the game and have fun and not worry so much about winning. Some leagues don't even keep score. Coaches usually try to play everyone an equal amount.

Travel Soccer

The term "travel soccer" means different things to different people, and that's mostly because there is such a huge range of leagues, all with their own guidelines. But one thing they all have in common is that the teams travel to other towns to play.

Some travel teams are formed through tryouts. They try to get the best players possible, and their goal is to win.

Many of these travel teams hire professional trainers to coach the players, and they definitely have several practices a week, in addition to games and tournaments. For an elite player, this option probably offers the best way to improve, but if you're on the bubble, you might find yourself sitting on the bench for an elite team. There's also no guarantee that you'll be on the team. Most elite teams have tryouts first. If your team has tryouts, here are some things you can do to make a good impression:

1. Come prepared. Make a checklist the day before tryouts detailing everything you need to bring. Socks, shoes, shin guards, water, a special shirt, shorts, etc. Check each item off right before you leave for the tryouts.

2. Be prompt. Coaches like players who arrive on time and ready to play. Don't show up right when tryouts start and begin getting ready. If you need the time to put on your shin guards and shoes, arrive early. Also, this will give you some extra time to warm up and calm your nerves.

3. Be positive. No matter what happens during tryouts, maintain a positive attitude and be enthusiastic. Be someone the coach wants to have on his team.

4. Work with the other players. Soccer is a team game! Don't be so busy showing off your own skill that you forget that there are other players on the field.

5. Bring on the moves. Your coach will be impressed with your new ball-handling tricks. Don't be afraid to show them off—just don't be a ball hog.

6. Be a good listener. Coaches want players that can listen and learn.

7. Relax and have fun! You're trying out for the team because you love soccer. Going to tryouts shouldn't be a chore. Rather, it allots you a couple of hours to have some fun playing a game that you enjoy. Coaches like a player with a love of the game.

Some other travel teams are less competitive. They join leagues where the level of play is lower, and they may have rules about equal playing time. This level of travel soccer varies tremendously. Some have professional trainers as coaches, and some have parents as coaches. Some have tryouts, and some just sign players up and divide them into teams.

As you can see, there are lots of different ways to find a team. If you're lucky, your town or city will offer several options. Then it's up to you to do the research and find out which type of league works best for you. If you aren't able to choose, then take what you have and make the most of it. You can always push yourself even if your team or league isn't pushing you.

Soccer-gram

Fill in the answers to the clues, one letter in each numbered space. Then transfer the letters to the boxes above that have the same numbers. When all the boxes are filled correctly, you will have the answer to this riddle:

YUCK!

SQUISH

Why is a soccer field often wet?

A. _ _ _ Easily frighened; timid
  10 2 7

B. _ _ _ _ _ Woman on her wedding day
  20 9 19 17 3

C. _ _ _ What a spider builds
  13 8 21

D. _ _ _ _ _ One thickness of something
  5 11 15 23 18

E. _ _ Short nickname for father
  4 14

F. _ _ _ _ _ Place in a barn for a horse
  16 1 6 12 22

1	2	3		4	5	6	7	8	9	10		11	12	13	14	15	16		17	18	19	20	21	22	23

!

Playing for Your School

Most high schools, and many middle schools, have soccer teams for both boys and girls. These are usually highly competitive teams, with both tryouts and a tough practice and game schedule. But if you love soccer, then this is exactly what you're hoping for!

And then after that there are college teams to play for. And then professional teams. But the ultimate prize for either a man or a woman is the national team. The national teams are made up of the top 20 players in a country, and they represent the country in international competitions, such as the Olympics and World Cup.

FUN FACT

Where Are You From?

Players have to be citizens of the country they play for, but they don't have to have been born there. On the 1998 U.S. National Team, one player became a U.S. citizen only a week before the World Cup began!

FUN FACT

Let's Share

A lot of countries aren't capable of handling the crowds or the matches of the World Cup, but they still want to host. In the 2002 World Cup, Korea and Japan solved the problem by sharing hosting duties. Each country had ten cities hosting games.

World Cup Soccer

The World Cup is an international competition that is held every four years. In the United States, the Super Bowl and the World Series are bigger events, but worldwide, the World Cup is the number one sporting competition. Roughly 200 countries compete to be the top soccer team in the world.

As you can imagine, the World Cup is a pretty big undertaking. Trying to narrow down 200 countries into one final winner takes a lot of time and involves tons of matches. The years in between each World Cup are spent qualifying for the next one. Only 32 of those original 200 countries get to go.

So who are the lucky ones? Well, first of all, the country who hosts the World Cup automatically gets in, so countries are very eager to be the hosts. FIFA moves the Cup all over the world to make it fair, but it is a huge undertaking to host such a competition and not every country is able to provide the stadiums and handle the crowds. Germany hosted in 2006, South Africa is hosting in 2010, and Brazil will host in 2014.

So, the host team is one team of the 32. Then the defending champions from the previous World Cup automatically get in. That's two. The rest of the teams have to earn one of the remaining 30 spots by playing qualifying matches.

FIFA divides the world into 10 divisions. Then each team in that division plays qualifying matches against the other teams in that division. When the matches are all done, the top three teams in each division qualify for the World Cup—in addition to the other 30 teams.

Then the World Cup begins. The teams are divided into eight groups with four teams each. FIFA looks at the scores and the win/loss records of all the qualifying matches and then spreads the top teams throughout the eight groups, so they aren't all playing each other in the first round.

Finally it's summer, and it's time for the World Cup competition to begin. The first round of the tournament is played as a round robin. Each team plays the other three teams in the group. The two teams that come out of that little competition with the best record move on. So, do the math. How many are eliminated and how many move on? If you guess 16 for both, you're right!

Now it's single-elimination time. The winner of group A plays the runner-up of group B. The winner of group B plays the runner-up of group A. The winner of group C plays the runner-up of group D, and so on. The teams play one game, and the winners of that game move on. Now we're down to eight teams, and it's single elimination the rest of the way until there's one final winner.

Here are the winning countries since the World Cup began in 1930:

WORDS to KNOW

Qualifying matches: Soccer games between countries to determine the top thirty soccer teams in the world for the World Cup.

- ◆ 1930: Uruguay
- ◆ 1934: Italy
- ◆ 1938: Italy
- ◆ 1942: No World Cup because of World War II
- ◆ 1946: No World Cup because of World War II
- ◆ 1950: Uruguay
- ◆ 1954: West Germany
- ◆ 1958: Brazil
- ◆ 1962: Brazil
- ◆ 1966: England
- ◆ 1970: Brazil
- ◆ 1974: West Germany
- ◆ 1978: Argentina
- ◆ 1982: Italy
- ◆ 1986: Argentina
- ◆ 1990: Germany
- ◆ 1994: Brazil
- ◆ 1998: France
- ◆ 2002: Brazil
- ◆ 2006: Italy

The Women's World Cup began in 1991, so it is much newer. Also, participation in women's sports is still growing around the world, so there aren't as many countries competing. The first two years of the Women's World Cup, there were only 12 countries participating. In 1999, however, it jumped to 16 teams, and the fan base has been growing every year.

FUN FACT

World Cup Groupings

The qualifying teams find out their group about six months before the World Cup. Then they're not allowed to play the other three teams in their group until the World Cup. They usually try to set up matches with teams that have similar styles, though.

World Cup Crossword

Figure out the answers to the questions below and fill them into the numbered crossword grid. All the answers will have to do with the great soccer info you learned while enjoying this book!

ACROSS

1. "_____ makes perfect!"
4. You can easily trap the ball here (between the head and the waist).
7. Short pass made using the inside of the foot (2 words).
10. If you get a _____ card, you are out of the game!
11. Keeping your body between the ball and another team's player.
14. Playing soccer is a lot of _____!
15. "I'm at a right angle to you!"
16. If you are attacking the goal, you are on _____.
20. Oops! You are between the opponent and the ball, and you're not going for the ball!
23. The most important soccer drink.
24. Look like you're going left, but you are really going right.
25. The other kids you play soccer with.
27. The ultimate soccer trophy (2 words).
28. The most important piece of soccer equipment.
29. What the ref blows.
30. "I'm behind you!"
31. Another name for the goalie.

DOWN

1. Most famous soccer player from Brazil.
2. To get a flying ball under control, you must _____ it.
3. Ouch! You stretched a ligament and have a bad _____.
5. Another name for an instep pass is a _____ pass."
6. When a player kicks the ball out of the air.
8. These keep the part of your leg below the knee safe.
9. Jesters do this with three balls, but soccer players do it with only one!
12. The most basic soccer rule: NO _____!
13. If you're protecting the goal, you're on _____.
17. Another name for a "forward."
18. What they call soccer in other countries.
19. A player might run _____ miles in a soccer game!
21. Do this to keep your muscles flexible and soft.
22. If you knock the ball over your own goal line, the other team gets a _____ (2 words).
24. Action that is not allowed.
26. Don't wait! Rush up to _____ the ball.
27. Initials for the women's professional soccer league.

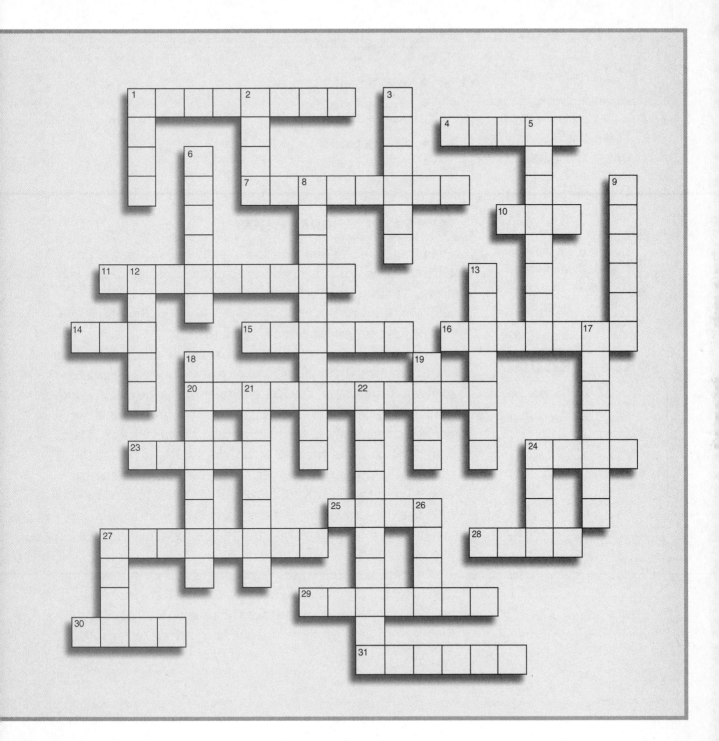

JOKIN' AROUND

Some flies were playing football in a saucer, using a sugar lump as a ball.

One of them said, "We'll have to do better than this, lads. We're playing in the cup tomorrow."

Here are the winning countries for the Women's World Cup:

◆ 1991: United States
◆ 1995: Norway
◆ 1999: United States
◆ 2003: Germany
◆ 2007: Germany

Men's Professional Soccer

Even though we've had a national team since 1916, the United States is viewed as a newcomer to the professional soccer scene. That's mostly because we haven't been very good. In addition, until recently there hasn't been a good professional league for our best players to compete in.

Throughout the twentieth century, a few different leagues were established, but none met with any great success. The big break came when the United States was awarded hosting job for the 1994 World Cup. Having its own professional soccer league was part of the hosting deal, so lucky for us, Major League Soccer was born. MLS was careful not to repeat the mistakes of the earlier leagues. They started small, and they also limited the number of players from other countries—only five non–U.S. citizens were allowed on each team. The league began with 10 teams, and the first game was played in 1996.

Overall, MLS can be seen as a success. Most of the teams have devoted fans. Some cities have dropped their teams, but new ones have come to take their place. Now MLS has 14 teams, with Seattle to join in 2009 and Philadelphia in 2010.

Eastern Division

The Eastern division of the MLS is made up of the following teams:

- Chicago Fire
- Columbus Crew
- D.C. United
- Kansas City Wizards
- New England Revolution
- New York Red Bulls
- Toronto FC

Western Division

The Western division is composed of:

- FC Dallas
- Los Angeles Galaxy
- Colorado Rapids
- Real Salt Lake
- San Jose Earthquakes
- Chivas USA
- Houston Dynamo

Major League Soccer games are fun to watch. Most of them are played in a small stadium, so you can get close to the action. It's a great way to pick up soccer tips and have a fun time, too.

Women's Professional Soccer

Women's soccer in the United States has a pretty short history, but what they lack in years, they've certainly made up in

FUN FACT

And the Winner Is...

On April 6, 1996, the MLS played its first game. The San Jose Clash went up against D.C. United. It was as exciting as the founders had hoped, a nail biter to the end. The score was 0–0 up until the last two minutes when the Clash's Eric Wynalda scored, giving the Clash the league's first victory. The Clash are now known as the San Jose Earthquakes. But D.C. United won at the end of the season by being the first winners of the MLS Cup.

JOKIN' AROUND

Question: How do the MLS teams stay cool in the summer?
Answer: They use their fans.

WORDS to KNOW

Title IX: A law passed in 1972 requiring schools to provide equal sports opportunity for girls and boys.

ability. Until 1972, when Title IX (Title 9) was made into law, there weren't many sports options for girls. There were a few sports (such as field hockey), but soccer usually wasn't one of them.

But then in the seventies, things started to change. Towns were realizing that soccer was cheap in terms of equipment and an easy sport for kids to learn. Youth leagues started popping up everywhere. Because of Title IX, there were opportunities for both girls and boys to play. And the girls were off and running.

It turns out that girls all over the world were starting to realize the same thing. This sport is fun! Women's teams started to develop and the level of skill skyrocketed. In 1991, FIFA created the first Women's World Cup. Guess who won? Yup, the United States.

When the United States women won the Women's World Cup in 1999, they attracted more attention, more TV viewers, and more fans than any other women's sport in history. Many people felt that this was the time to start a women's professional soccer league: the WUSA (which stood for Women's United Soccer Association). The first game was played on April 14, 2001, between the Bay Area Cyber Rays and the Washington Freedom (Washington won), but the league folded after only two seasons.

Women's soccer couldn't be held down, though. A new group formed and created WPS (Women's Professional Soccer) in 2007, creating a new seven-team league that will have its first games in 2009. Two more teams (Atlanta and Philadelphia) plan to join the league in 2010. Here are the teams. Some have already decided on their names, but some haven't yet:

- ◆ Boston Breakers
- ◆ Chicago Red Stars
- ◆ Dallas

112

- Los Angeles
- NJ/NY Sky Blue Soccer
- St. Louis
- Washington Freedom

Do you have a team near you? Go out and support them, so that this league will become a big success! If women's soccer turns out to be a big hit, what other cities around the country would be good places for the women's league to expand? List five cities and come up with good names to go with them. Maybe WPS will take your suggestions!

_____

_____

_____

_____

_____

If you don't have a WPS team near you, you can watch some of their games on television. Watching the pros play will definitely help you improve your game. Then maybe someday you can be the one on TV.

So you're a master at the game now, right? You're a dynamite dribbler, a shooting star, a perfect passer, a terrific trapper, and an awesome attacker. You've perfected your play, beaten your buddies, and even wrapped up reading this book. Or you might be a beginner who is thinking that this is the perfect sport for you. Or maybe you're just a big fan of World Cup Soccer. No matter what makes you love soccer, there are many ways to enjoy the world's favorite sport. You don't have to look far to find a way to get your kicks out of soccer!

FUN FACT

A Woman's Game

The first record of a women's game was one played in Scotland in the 1600s. This was a game between married women and unmarried women. The married women won.

APPENDIX A

Glossary

attacker
A player whose main job is to shoot on the opponent's goal.

chip
A sharp, stabbing kick that gives the ball some backspin but doesn't give much distance, so the player is able to loft the ball over an opponent's head without the ball going too far.

concussion
An injury to the head, particularly the brain, usually involving loss of consciousness and dizziness.

containment
The process of slowing down an attacker and keeping him in front of you as you back toward the goal.

corner kick
The free kick given to the attacking team when the defending team has kicked the ball over its own end line.

cross
A pass from the sideline into the center of the field in front of the goal.

defender
A player whose main job is to protect her own goal.

dehydration
A serious lack of water in your body that can cause a dangerous health situation.

direct kick
The free kick given to a team when a player on the other team has committed a foul. This kick may go directly into the goal.

dribbling
A series of short, crisp taps on the ball that allows the soccer player to run with the ball under his control.

electrolytes
Ions in your body that control the flow of water throughout the cells.

FIFA
The Fédération Internationale de Football Association is the official soccer organization for world play. If a rule change is made, it's made by FIFA.

follow through
A term used in many sports. It means that the swinging motion doesn't stop with impact. The leg (or baseball bat or tennis racket) continues to move forward in the same direction.

give-and-go

It is a way of getting around a defender by "bouncing" the ball off one of your teammates. Your teammate receives the ball while you run around the defender and then passes it back to you when you're free.

goalkeeper

The only player on the field allowed to use his hands. This ability is restricted to the penalty-box area.

goal kick

The free kick awarded to the defending team when the attacking team has kicked the ball over the goal line.

goal line

Also known as the end line. One of the two shorter lines that form the boundaries of the field of play. The lines are included as part of the field.

half-volley

A shot in which the player kicks the ball after it has bounced. The ball is still in the air but only a bit off the ground.

header

when a player uses his head to direct the ball.

indirect kick

The free kick given to a team when a player on the other team has committed a foul. This kick must be touched by two players before it can go into the goal.

instep

The arched middle portion of the foot directly in front of the ankle and under the shoelaces.

instep pass

Or shoelace pass. A powerful pass that lets the player loft the ball into the air by striking it with her instep.

juggling

Keeping the ball from touching the ground using your feet and thighs and even your head to pop the ball back up into the air.

kickoff

The free kick that begins the game and the second half. It is also the way play is restarted after a goal has been scored.

ligaments

The connectors between your bones. Ligaments also support organs and connect cartilage to bones.

marking up

Another term for man-to-man defense. That means you cover a player rather than an area, staying with him no matter where he goes.

midfielder

A transition position between attack and defense.

MLS

Major League Soccer. The MLS is the professional men's soccer league in the United States.

obstruction

This call means you've placed your body between your opponent and the ball without going after the ball yourself. You might be trying to keep your opponent from saving the ball if it's going out-of-bounds or to give your keeper a chance to pick it up. Either way, it's not allowed. You can throw your body in front of another player, however, as long as you're actually going after the ball.

offsides

A violation of the rule that requires either the ball or two defenders be between an attacker and the goal.

penalty box

The area in front of the goal inside the 18-yard line.

penalty kick

A free kick awarded when the defending team fouls inside the penalty box.

plant

A step toward the ball that shifts your weight forward and gives you more power for your kick.

push pass

A short accurate pass using the inside of the foot.

qualifying matches

Soccer games between countries to determine the top 30 soccer teams in the world.

restart

Occurs after play has been stopped because of the referee's whistle. Restarts include corner kicks, goal kicks, direct kicks, indirect kicks, kickoffs, and throw-ins.

RICE

The acronym to help remember the treatment of rest, ice, compression, and elevation for injuries.

shielding

The process of keeping your body between the defender and the ball to prevent the defender from getting to the ball.

sprain

A stretching or tearing of a ligament.

stopper

A position considered the first line of defense.

striker

Another term for the center forward.

sweeper
A position considered the last line of defense.

Title IX
A law passed in 1972 that essentially said that schools couldn't have a sport for boys and not have one for girls if there was an interest.

throw-in
The method of returning the ball to play when it has gone over the touchline.

touchline
Also known as the sideline. One of the two longer lines that are the boundaries of the field of play. The lines are included as part of the field of play.

trapping
Stopping the soccer ball and getting it under control with any part of the body.

volley
A shot in which the player kicks the ball out of the air.

World Cup
The ultimate soccer trophy. The team that wins the World Cup competition is considered the best soccer team in the world.

WPS
Women's Professional Soccer.

zone defense
Covering an area rather than a person. You pick up the player who goes into that area.

117

Web Resources

FIFA

The Fédération Internationale de Football Association is the organization in charge of international soccer, with 208 member countries. It is located in Zurich, Switzerland.

Visit FIFA's website for up-to-the-minute news and fun facts about all your favorite soccer teams.

www.fifa.com

World Cup

If it's the World Cup that you're most interested in, you can click on these links. They are part of FIFA's website, but it saves you the trouble of navigating through all the rest of the information:

www.fifa.com/worldcup
www.fifa.com/womensworldcup

United States Soccer

If you want to know more about the United States men's or women's national teams, you're in luck. They have a website that will give you information on rosters, upcoming games, and even the history of the teams. You can also buy tickets, merchandise, and join their fan club.

www.ussoccer.com

Major League Soccer (MLS)

If you love finding out the latest news about D.C. United, the New York Red Bulls, or the San Jose Earthquakes, go to the MLS website for all the news in Major League Soccer. They have reports on each game, profiles of your favorite players, and much, much more.

www.mlsnet.com

Women's Professional Soccer (WPS)

If you want to join in the excitement about the new women's professional league, then head straight for their website.

www.womensprosoccer.com

Soccer America

Soccer America is a magazine that will keep you up to date on all the soccer issues in this country. It also touches on key World Cup issues and some interesting developments in international soccer. You can order the magazine itself or read some of the articles online. The website might also give you a free trial subscription.

www.socceramerica.com

The Soccer Hall of Fame

The Soccer Hall of Fame in the United States is in Oneanta, NY, but you can find it online, along with all the stats and stories on the famous players from the past.

www.soccerhalloffame.org

Collectibles

If you're the kind of soccer fan who not only loves to play the game but also loves to collect sports cards of all your favorite professional soccer players, then there's a great website for you and it has any soccer card you could ever imagine wanting.

www.soccercards.com

Tryout Tips

Are you worried about upcoming tryouts? Nothing is more intimidating than lining up with a bunch of other kids who are getting ready to show off their soccer skills. Who plays which position? Have they been training? What secrets do they know about the game that you don't? Relax! Every other person there is wrestling with the same uncertainties and nerves.

Tips for a Great Tryout

Relax. You know that you have great skills if you perform to the best of your abilities. Keep that in mind and take a deep breath. Now go out and give it your best effort. Remember, nerves have an uncanny ability to cause mistakes. Coaches will take that into consideration, but do your best to keep those butterflies in your stomach still!

Be positive. No matter what happens during tryouts, maintain a positive attitude and disposition. If you make a mistake, ask the coach for advice. Analyze the play and see what you can do to make sure that the mistake isn't repeated. Everyone makes mistakes. However, players that shake it off and keep working hard show a maturity and sportsmanship that is admired by everyone.

Work with the other players. Soccer is a game that requires teamwork. Don't be so busy showing off your own skill that you forget that there are other players on the field. No one likes a ball hog. Use your ability to work with your teammates. If your teammate has a better shot, pass the ball. This shows smart playing. After all, you're all after the same goal!

Get in shape. If you can show your coach that you've been working hard on your own time, it will reflect well in tryouts. Coaches are looking for kids that are dedicated enough to stay in shape. Plus, it doesn't hurt to be the first one to finish a fitness test!

Bring on the moves. Your coach will be impressed with your new ball-handling tricks. Don't be afraid to show them off. Remember, soccer is a game of both skill and smarts. If you can show the coach that you know the game, recognize the strategy, and can play intelligently, the lasting impression is sure to be a positive one.

Get enough sleep. We all know that an early bedtime is for younger kids, but if you want to succeed in the tryouts, you need to be on top of your game. Get plenty of sleep the night before tryouts to ensure that you're well rested and ready to play a good game of soccer. A good night's sleep will keep you alert, energized, and positive throughout the tryouts.

Be a good listener. Coaches want players that can listen and learn. Listen closely when your coach gives you instruction. He or she may be testing your ability to understand simple instructions.

Be prompt. Coaches like players who arrive on time and ready to play. Don't show up right when tryouts start and begin getting ready. If you need the time to put on your shin guards and shoes, arrive early. Also, this will give you some extra time to warm up and calm your nerves.

Be willing to try new things. If the coach asks you to try a drill you've never done, let alone never heard of, be open and willing to try it. If you don't understand, ask questions. A coach is there to help you learn and improve. Be willing to try a new move, or a new shot on the goal. You may even find that you like it!

Be health-conscious. Make sure that you eat a nutritious meal a few hours before the tryouts, and bring lots of water. You'll need the water to stay hydrated and alert.

Come prepared. Make a checklist the day before tryouts detailing everything you need to bring. Socks, shoes, shin guards, water, a special shirt, shorts, etc. Check it off right before you leave for the tryouts. Coming prepared makes a good impression on any coach.

Be friendly. Part of what makes a great team is how everyone works together. Be nice to the other players, get to know them, and help out when asked. Coaches appreciate players with a positive attitude who are friendly with each other. If you don't know all of the other players, introduce yourself. Strike up a conversation. You can always ask the person where she's from, what position she plays, or if she's nervous, too! You may find that you've got a new friend.

Have fun! You're trying out for the team because you love soccer. Going to tryouts shouldn't be a chore. Rather, it allots you a couple of hours to have some fun playing a game that you enjoy. Coaches like a player that has a love of the game. This indicates a willingness to learn and succeed.

National Soccer Hall of Famers

I f you practice really hard, maybe someday your name will end up on this list! These Hall of Fame players are not chosen from skill alone, but also for their integrity, sportsmanship, and character—both on and off the field.

1950
Jock Ferguson
Billy Gonsalves
Sheldon Govier
Millard Lang
Robert Millar
Harry Ratican
Dick Spalding
Archie Stark
Peter Wilson

1951
Harold Brittan
Davey Brown
William Fryer
John McGuire
Robert Morrison
Peter Renzulli
Thomas Swords

1952
George Tintle

1953
Jimmy Douglas
John Jaap

1954
Aldo "Buff" Donelli

1955
Thomas Duggan

1958
Francis Ryan

1959
Ralph Carrafi

1963
Rudy Kuntner

1965
Fred Beardsworth
Teddy Glover

1966
Stan Chesney

1968
Arnie Oliver

1971
Gene Olaff
Bert Patenaude

1973
Joseph Gryzik

1974
Nick DiOrio
Jimmy Dunn
Werner Mieth

1976
Walter Bahr
Frank Borghi
Charlie Colombo
Geoff Coombes
Robert Craddock Jr.
Joe Gaetjens
Gino Gard
Harry Keough
Joseph Maca
Edward McIlvenny
Gino Pariani
Edward Souza
John Souza
Frank Wallace
Adam Wolanin

1977
Jack Hynes
Ben McLaughlin

1978
Raymond Bernabei
Al Zerhusen

1979
Al Harker

1980
John Boulos

1982
Joseph Carenza

1983
George Barr

1986
Andrew Auld
Mike Bookie
James Brown
Thomas Florie
Jimmy Gallagher
James Gentle
Bart McGhee
George Moorhouse
Philip Slone
Ralph Tracey
Frank Vaughn
Alexander Wood

1989
Walter Dick
Bob Gormley
Werner Roth
Willy Roy

1990
Shamus O'Brien

1991
Rudy Getzinger

1992
Chico Chacurian
Werner Fricker

1993
John Nanoski
Pelé

1994
Pat McBride
Lloyd Monsen

1995
Robert Annis
George Brown
Willy Schaller

1996
Nick Kropfelder
Len Oliver

1997
Paul Danilo
Alex Ely
Johnny Moore
Jimmy Roe

1998
F. Beckenbauer
April Heinrichs
Ed Murphy

2000
Giorgio Chinaglia
Carin Jennings

2001
Rick Davis
Bill Looby

2002
Adolph Bachmeier
Vladislav "Bogie" Bogicevic
Shannon Higgins

2003
Carlos Alberto Torres
Paul Child
Karl-Heinz Granitza
Bobby Lenarduzzi
Arnie Mausser
Patrick "Ace'" Ntsoelengoe

Alan Willey
Bruce Wilson

2004
Michelle Akers
Paul Caligiuri
Michael Windischmann
Eric Wynalda

2005
Marcelo Balboa
Fernando Clavijo
Tom "Whitey'"Fleming
John Harkes
Alex McNab
John Nelson
Werner Nilsen
Tab Ramos
Fabri Salcedo

2006
Alexi Lalas
Carla Overbeck
Al Trost

2007
Julie Foudy
Mia Hamm
Bobby Smith

2008
Hugo Perez

APPENDIX E

Puzzle Answers

page 6 ◆ **Spelling Ball**

ALIVE	PAL(S)	SILVER
EVIL	PALE	SLAP
LAP	PALER	SLIVER
LEAP	PERT	TOIL
LION	PET	TOIL
LIVE	REAL	TON
LIVER	REAP	VELVET
NOISE	REAPER	VETO
NOT	RELIVE	VISION
NOTE	REVOTE	VOTE
OVER	SEAL	VOTER

10-letter bonus word: TELEVISION

page 12 ◆ **Let's Play**

1. CLOCK
2. FIELD
3. REFEREE
4. BALL
5. TEAM
6. WHISTLE

BONUS: CLEATS

page 20 ◆ **Skill Master**

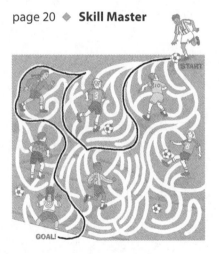

page 22 ◆ **Skill Master Questions**

1. 7
2. 4
3. spiral
4. top left corner

Bonus: 8 and 3

Puzzle Answers

page 26 ◆ **Speed Drill**
Answer: wide open

page 27 ◆ **I Spy Soccer**

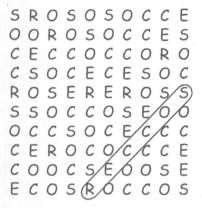

```
S R O S O S O C C E
O O R O S O C C E S
C E C C O C C O R O
C S O C E C E S O C
R O S E R E R O S S
S S O C C O S E O O
O C C S O C E C C C
C E R O C O C C C E
C O O C S E O O S E
E C O S R O C C O S
```

page 31 ◆ **Speed Drill**
Answer: a plant

page 38 ◆ **Teamwork**

A	B	
~~YEE~~	BID	EYELID
ORF	ROT	FORBID
NPA	AGE	PANTRY
ONT	FIT	NOTICE
RAC	TRY	CARROT
OTC	~~LID~~	COTTON
AMN	ICE	MANAGE
UTO	TON	OUTFIT

page 44 ◆ **Practice, Practice, Practice**

B	F		T		O		T	I	T	E		O	C		E		P	U			3
I	E	S	N	D	O	A	F	G	H	T	E	S	O	U	C	R	Y	O	O	A	E	I	Y
D	H	E	Y	O	U	T	D	O	O	H	E	D	F	G	N	A	A	N	T	E	L	B	L	L
T	A	Y	A	E	S	W	R	F	I	T	T	H	S	I	M	O	R	T	H	R	W	H	L	E	W	E	R	O
I	F		Y	O	U		D	O		T	H	I	S		F	O	R		A		W	H	O	L	E		3	0
D	A	Y	S		S	T	R	A	I	G	H	T	,	I		G	U	A	R	A	N	T	E	E		B	Y
T	H	E		E	N	D		O	F		T	H	E		M	O	N	T	H		Y	O	U		W	I	L	L
B	E		A		T	W	O	-	F	O	O	T	E	D		S	O	C	C	E	R		P	L	A	Y	E	R

page 34 ◆ **Fast Pass**

START

GOAL!

page 49 ◆ **Keep Your Eye on the Ball**

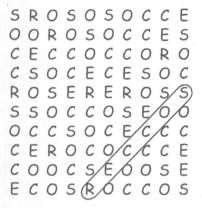

126

page 54 ◆ **Uniform Uniforms**

page 59 ◆ **Speed Drill**
Answer: in the box

page 62 ◆ **We're with You!**

W A Y T O GO, GOALIE !

page 69 ◆ **Move the Ball**

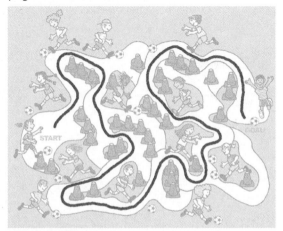

page 72 ◆ **Speed Drill**
Answer: meet the ball

page 75 ◆ **Opposite Offense**

"Hey ~~here~~ there, Lucas!"

"~~Good-bye~~ Hello, Caitlin!"

"How are ~~me~~ you?"

"~~You haven't~~ I have a ~~good~~ bad ~~hot~~ cold."

"How ~~wonderful~~ awful! I

hope you ~~give~~ get ~~worse~~ better

~~a long time from now~~ soon."

"~~You~~ Me, too. I ~~did~~ didn't ~~wake~~ sleep

~~none~~ all ~~day~~ night ~~short~~ long."

"Oh, that's too ~~good~~ bad.

Well, ~~you~~ I ~~haven't~~ have to

~~come~~ go. ~~Hello~~ goodye!"

"~~Hello~~ Good-bye. See ~~me~~ you ~~sooner~~ later."

page 76 ◆ **Super Soccer**

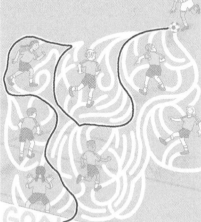

page 78 ◆ **Speed Drill**
Answer: one on one

page 80 ◆ **Speed Drill**
Answer: the wall

Puzzle Answers

page 84 ◆ Defensive Lineup

The goalie, Josh, is the tallest.
The wing is Flo.
The fullback is Jamal.
The sweeper is Ben.
The stopper, Patty, is the shortest.

page 86 ◆ Go Team!

WE GET A
KICK OUT
OF SOCCER

page 95 ◆ Body Building

1. Twelve inches	foot	
2. They hold up a chair	Legs	
3. Two units of corn	ears	
4. Hiding place for treasure	chest	
5. A baby cow	calf	
6. A tropical tree	palm	
7. Part of a comb	tooth	
8. There are two on a clock	hands	
9. Needles have threads in them	eyes	
10. A unit of lettuce	head	

page 90 ◆ Warm Up

Puzzle Answers

page 98 ◆ Secret Soccer

```
S R O S O S O C C E
O O R O S O C C E S
C E C C O C C O R O
C S O C E C E S O C
R O S E R E R O S S
S S O C C O S E O O
O C C S O C E C C C
C E R O C O C C C E
C O O C S E O O S E
E C O S R O C C O S
```

page 105 ◆ Soccer-gram

A. $\underset{10}{S}$ $\underset{2}{H}$ $\underset{7}{Y}$ Easily frighened; timid

B. $\underset{20}{B}$ $\underset{9}{R}$ $\underset{19}{I}$ $\underset{17}{D}$ $\underset{3}{E}$ Woman on her wedding day

C. $\underset{13}{W}$ $\underset{8}{E}$ $\underset{21}{B}$ What a spider builds

D. $\underset{5}{L}$ $\underset{11}{A}$ $\underset{15}{Y}$ $\underset{23}{E}$ $\underset{18}{R}$ One thickness of something

E. $\underset{4}{P}$ $\underset{14}{A}$ Short nickname for father

F. $\underset{16}{S}$ $\underset{1}{T}$ $\underset{6}{A}$ $\underset{12}{L}$ $\underset{22}{L}$ Place in a barn for a horse

THE PLAYERS ALWAYS DRIBBLE!

page 100 ◆ Playing for Real

```
C P V O L L E Y T S
R A L O C C E R K D
R E T A I S A I D E
E K C C N P C R A F
L N L E H K I L A E
G I B O I B U T C N
U H O P B V E N N D
J T A L T R E K U O
J S E S H O O T A R
S L H C T E R T S F
```

Extra letters spell:
Soccer is all about control!

page 109 ◆ World Cup Crossword

129

Index

The Everything® KIDS' Series!

Packed with tons of information, activities, and puzzles, the Everything® Kids' books are perennial bestsellers that keep kids active and engaged.

Each book is $7.95, two-color, 8" x 9¼", and 144 –176 pages.

The Everything® Kids'
Cookbook, 2nd Ed.
ISBN 10: 1-59869-592-4

The Everything® Kids' Dragons
Puzzle and Activity Book
ISBN 10: 1-59869-623-8

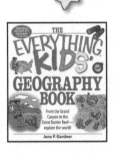

The Everything® Kids'
Geography Book
ISBN 10: 1-59869-683-1

The Everything® Kids' Hanukkah
Puzzle and Activity Book
ISBN 10: 1-59869-788-9

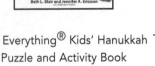

The Everything® Kids' Money
Book, 2nd Ed.
ISBN 10: 1-59869-784-6

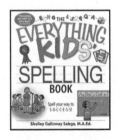

The Everything® Kids' Mummies,
Pharaohs, and Pyramids Puzzle
and Activity Book
ISBN 10: 1-59869-797-8

The Everything® Kids'
Spelling Book
ISBN 10: 1-59869-754-4

A silly, goofy, and undeniably icky addition to
the Everything® Kids' series . . .

The Everything® Kids'

GROSS

Series

Chock—full of sickening entertainment for hours of disgusting fun.

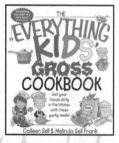

The Everything® Kids'
Gross Cookbook
1-59869-324-7, $7.95

The Everything® Kids' Gross
Hidden Pictures Book
1-59337-615-4, $7.95

The Everything® Kids'
Gross Jokes Book
1-59337-448-8, $7.95

The Everything® Kids'
Gross Mazes Book
1-59337-616-2, $7.95

The Everything® Kids' Gross
Puzzle & Activity Book
1-59337-447-X, $7.95

Other Everything® Kids' Titles Available

The Everything® Kids' Animal Puzzle & Activity Book
1-59337-305-8

The Everything® Kids' Astronomy Book
1-59869-544-4

The Everything® Kids' Baseball Book, 5th Ed.
1-59869-487-1

The Everything® Kids' Bible Trivia Book
1-59337-031-8

The Everything® Kids' Bugs Book
1-58062-892-3

The Everything® Kids' Cars and Trucks
Puzzle and Activity Book
1-59337-703-7

The Everything® Kids' Christmas Puzzle
& Activity Book
1-58062-965-2

The Everything® Kids' Connect the Dots Puzzle and Activity
Book
1-59869-647-5

The Everything® Kids' Crazy Puzzles Book
1-59337-361-9

The Everything® Kids' Dinosaurs Book
1-59337-360-0

The Everything® Kids' Environment Book
1-59869-670-X

The Everything® Kids' Fairies Puzzle and Activity Book
1-59869-394-8

The Everything® Kids' First Spanish Puzzle and
Activity Book
1-59337-717-7

The Everything® Kids' Football Book
1-59869-565-7

The Everything® Kids' Halloween Puzzle &
Activity Book
1-58062-959-8

The Everything® Kids' Hidden Pictures Book
1-59337-128-4

The Everything® Kids' Horses Book
1-59337-608-1

The Everything® Kids' Joke Book
1-58062-686-6

The Everything® Kids' Knock Knock Book
1-59337-127-6

The Everything® Kids' Learning French Book
1-59869-543-6

The Everything® Kids' Learning Spanish Book
1-59337-716-9

The Everything® Kids' Magical Science Experiments Book
1-59869-426-X

The Everything® Kids' Math Puzzles Book
1-58062-773-0

The Everything® Kids' Mazes Book
1-58062-558-4

The Everything® Kids' Nature Book
1-58062-684-X

The Everything® Kids' Pirates Puzzle and Activity Book
1-59337-607-3

The Everything® Kids' Presidents Book
1-59869-262-3

The Everything® Kids' Princess Puzzle and Activity Book
1-59337-704-5

The Everything® Kids' Puzzle Book
1-58062-687-4

The Everything® Kids' Racecars Puzzle and Activity Book
1-59869-243-7

The Everything® Kids' Riddles & Brain Teasers Book
1-59337-036-9

The Everything® Kids' Science Experiments Book
1-58062-557-6

The Everything® Kids' Sharks Book
1-59337-304-X

The Everything® Kids' Soccer Book
1-58062-642-4

The Everything® Kids' Spies Puzzle and Activity Book
1-59869-409-X

The Everything® Kids' States Book
1-59869-263-1

The Everything® Kids' Travel Activity Book
1-58062-641-6

The Everything® Kids' Word Search Puzzle and Activity
Book
1-59869-545-2

JUL 1 4 2014

All titles are $6.95 or $7.95 unless otherwise noted.

Available wherever books are sold!
To order, call 800-258-0929, or visit us at www.adamsmedia.com
Everything® and everything.com® are registered trademarks of F+W Publications, Inc.
Prices subject to change without notice.